MW00423695

Losing Control

How God Used Cancer and Infertility to Bring Me to the End of Myself

Pray BIG!

Ashley Hallford

Psalm 30:2

Ashley Hallford
with Stephanie Monroe

Losing Control

Published by KDP.
Printed in the U.S.A.
ISBN: 9781981033898

First Edition

I have tried to recreate events, locales and conversations from
my memories of them. In order to maintain their anonymity in
some instances I have changed the names of individuals and
places, I may have changed some identifying characteristics and
details such as physical properties, occupations and places of
residence.

https://www.ashleyhallford.com/
All scripture is taken from *The Holy Bible*, 1611 KJV.

Ashley

To my three loves – Harley, Gracie and Eli.
You are each an answer to prayer.

Stephanie

To Chad – For believing that I could

Table of Contents

Chapter 1
Anyone but Job

"Though he slay me, yet will I trust in him…" Job 13:15

I often think about Job. His name is synonymous with suffering, yet from what we can see, he only went through one major trial in his life. Granted, it was a doozy, but his entire life became associated with suffering because of one season. His response to God during the trial wasn't anger or resentment or desertion – it was simply to ask, "Why me?" While his physical possessions were restored and new children came along, I imagine the whole episode left his heart and soul bruised. You don't just get over something like that. It becomes a part of you and shapes everything in your life from that moment forward.

One thing is certain – no one wants to be compared with Job. All of your children dying…on the same day? Absolutely not. Fortune lost? Please, no. Accusatory friends? I'll pass. Boils from head to toe and coated in ash? No thanks. Spouse that recommends you curse God so you can die? Yikes. Place where it feels like God has handed you over to the devil and left you out to dry? Maybe that one hits a little closer to home than most of us care to admit.

During the whirlwind of being diagnosed with cancer, having a premature baby, the cancer progressing rapidly, and enduring months of treatments and medications, I didn't even have a chance to make a pile of sackcloth and ashes like Job did. Life whizzed by like a runaway mine cart. It wasn't until after the dust of treatments settled that I began to look at the whole experience with some margin of perspective.

Self-pity slowly ebbed its way into my heart, rising like a twisted root cracking through the foundation of a house. People would hear my story and respond with, "You poor thing!" and I would immediately think, "Yes, poor me! It was awful!" I began to focus on my suffering and pain. The avalanche of bad news that had crashed down on us in such a short time crushed our carefully-constructed, comfortable world. To make sense of it all, I wanted answers. I wanted reasons. Why did this happen? More specifically, why did this happen to *me*?

Being a concrete thinker, I tried to rationalize the situation to myself. I felt sure that there had to be a reason. Something had to have caused this to happen to me. My brain constructed a hamster wheel of analysis, and I flopped along with every spin. If C happened, then I just needed to figure out what A and B were.

See, my fragile faith had not been tested before cancer. I didn't have anything in my life to push against the flimsy wall of belief I had formed out of years of growing up in church. Even though I may not have said it out loud, somewhere in my soul I had formed this idea that bad things happen to bad people, and conversely, good things happen to good people. Do A and B, and you will get C. Go to church, keep the rules, live right, and things will work out for you and your family. Have you ever been there? Has your skewed version of the truth sounded so logical that you started to believe it?

The more I wrestled with the "why me" question, the more I began to believe Satan's subtly twisted lie that God's blessings came to good people. As my self-pity deepened and wound its tentacles around my heart, its darker stepsister, resentment, began to take hold. My heart ached as I looked at pictures of my son Harley's first-year milestones such as learning to roll over, sit up, crawl, and eat baby food for the first time. I saw pictures of us together in situations I couldn't even remember, birthdays and holidays when I had been too sick or drugged to comprehend what was going on around me. The excruciating physical pain paled in comparison to all the moments I had missed with my son and my husband.

During the years Harley was little, my prayers were a lot like Job's.

God, why? Why did you allow this to happen? I know You are good, but I just don't understand. I don't understand why you would take away time and memories with my son? I will never get those back. There will always be a gaping hole. This seems ugly to even say and think, but I just don't understand why this happened to me. We are good people. I've gone to church and read my Bible. I have tried to love people and serve You. Please, just tell me why this happened. Was it something I did or something I didn't do?

I look around and see so many people doing such awful things, yet they have good lives. People who cheat and steal to move up in the world have more money in the bank than we could ever dream to have. People who don't take care of their children seem to be able to repopulate like rabbits. We desperately want more children and yet we are told that it is not possible. None of it makes sense. Please help me. Help me see your plan. Help me see the point of all this.

All of this emotional and spiritual unrest came bubbling out one day after church onto my unsuspecting Sunday School teacher. We attend a church where people feel more like family, so conversations have a way of going deep quickly. He asked how things were going, and in a moment of complete honesty with him and myself, I blurted out: "I just don't understand why this happened to me."

He looked up from the paperwork on the lectern in front of him. His light blue shirt folded along the shoulder line as he leaned his forearms against the flat surface next to his Bible. The elongated pause hung in the air until he finally broke the silence.

"Well, why not you?"

His words cut through my self-pity, resentment, and doubt. They seared my soul like a branding iron on a new calf. I stammered to form a reply, but he continued.

"What makes you so good that this shouldn't have happened to you?"

See, what I had failed to understand is that in God's economy A + B doesn't equal C. If doing "good" things and living a "good" life were assurances against trials and physical suffering, then Abraham, Moses, Job, Jeremiah, Paul, and all of the apostles got it wrong. In a fallen world of sin and brokenness, no one is exempt from pain and suffering. Easy lives ended in Eden.

"Ashley," he continued, flipping the thin pages of his Bible, "listen to what Peter tells us in 1 Peter 4:12-13. 'Beloved, think it not strange concerning the fiery trial which is to try you, as though some strange thing happened to you; but rejoice, inasmuch as ye are partakers of Christ's sufferings; that when his glory shall be revealed, ye may be glad also with exceeding joy.' Ashley, Jesus told us to expect trouble in this world. It shouldn't surprise us when it happens. We should expect trials. I'm not sure why God chose this trial for you exactly. Maybe He knew that you would have a church and a family that could rally around you and pray. Someone else may not have had that. Honestly though, I think Peter answers your why question pretty well. Your joy in this situation will be seeing God's glory shine through it. You can sit around and wonder, 'Why me?' or you can share you story and let God's light shine through you. It's your choice."

Everything changed in that moment. I wish I could tell you that I saw God's purpose in my story from the beginning, but I didn't. If you stand two inches from a masterpiece, you will miss the beauty of the piece. It is often that way for us. It isn't until years later, that we can look back with perspective and see the beautiful tapestry God was weaving at the time.

Finally, I knew the reason why. Maybe it wasn't the answer I thought I had wanted, but it was an answer that breathed new life into my soul. God had repositioned my life in order to give Himself more glory. If David and I had continued in our easy, run of the mill life, we would have continued to walk in our own strength, leaving God in a box that we pulled out on Sundays. We would have done good things to be good people and would have been satisfied with the outcome.

However, Isaiah 64:6 clearly tells us that even our righteousness – all of the good things we do – is filthy rags. Rotten rags don't measure up so well when you start to ask the question, "Why do bad things happen to good people?" I was reminded that no one is good. We are all equal at the foot of the cross and all stand in complete need of Christ's redemption. I thought my life and deeds were good and worthy because I had measured them against the wrong standard. Against the holiness of God, none of us stand worthy of anything.

I slipped out of bed that night and fell on my knees. My short, spiky hair pressed against the sheets as I tucked my bare feet underneath me.

"God, I'm sorry." Bitter tears plunged down my cheeks as my fist pounded the carpet.

"I am so ashamed. I am sorry that I somehow thought that this story was all about me. From now on I will see my life through a different lens. I don't deserve an easy life just because I go to church. I don't deserve anything good, yet You have given me so much out of Your grace. Salvation, physical healing, a healthy son, an amazing husband, a loving family, loyal friends, and a church family that stood in the gap for me when I was utterly helpless and could offer nothing in return.

"I can't offer you anything but a pile of rags, yet you offer me everything. Christ in me is the hope of glory that I want to share. Not just that you healed me from cancer, but that you healed me from my sin – a diagnosis far deadlier than any cancer. My only purpose is to give You glory. Just like the moon can't claim any light of its own, it simply reflects the light that it has been given. I want to do that. I want to shine Your light from my life. I want you to take the ashes of this situation and make something beautiful. I pray this pain and suffering can be shaped into a platform to tell Your story in a way that I would have never had before. I will rejoice in the suffering I have to endure here, knowing that You will bring ultimate healing in Heaven one day."

My story is ultimately not about me, my family, my church, or my doctors. It is one of God's glory and His grace. It's about the power of prayers and faith, about seeing God in the midst of terrible sadness and heartache, and about finding His beauty in the midst of our ashes.

Chapter 2
Baby Bump

"I will praise thee; for I am fearfully and wonderfully made..." Ps. 139:14

April 2007

My heart beat wildly in my chest as I gripped the bathroom door knob, turning it only slightly before releasing it again to take one more deep breath. I fought to compose myself and twisted the knob again, letting the door ease open. From the top of the stairs I could see my husband, David, sitting on the bottom step, lacing up his boots. I battled to slow my breathing and appear normal.

My sudden nerves honestly surprised me a little. I like control, and I'm pretty good at anticipating events and outcomes. Even with something so natural, I could not simply relax and let nature take its course. Like all areas of my life, I wanted as much information as possible. Information calms my nerves and helps me focus. It's how I face any new endeavor or challenge – gather facts, make a plan, and work the plan. I charted my ovulation and knew my cycle well. My husband, David, often teased me about my research and piles of books. He joked that people had managed to have babies for years without math or graphs, but I brushed his quips aside and went right on plotting.

Since I had charted my ovulation well, I needed no pregnancy signs or symptoms. I had the day marked on my calendar – April 27 – right beside my mother-in-law's birthday. While I had fully anticipated the day I would take the pregnancy test, all of my info gathering failed to prepare me for a positive result.

Now, I started toward the top step, the carpet pressing between my freshly painted toenails. I clutched the little stick in my left hand, nestled against my lower back and gripped the handrail with the other hand. Lulu, our loving but overzealous Jack Russell Terrier, bounced around David's feet as he worked to finish tying his boots. My uncharacteristic, sloth-like pace down the stairs caught Lulu's attention. She cocked her head slightly as if to say, "Well, what are you up to?"

David, a fireman with the Cobb Country Fire Department, stood up and walked toward the kitchen to grab his travel mug, brimming with coffee, before he left for a 24-hour shift. Over the last year and a half, I had grown accustomed to his 24-hours-on, 48-hours-off shift work. He was in his dream job after always wanting to follow in his dad's footsteps and become a firefighter.

He strolled back into the living room, coffee cup in hand. "Ashley!" he called, as he reached down to wrestle briefly with Lulu, but as he stood up, his eyes landed on me at the bottom of the stairs.

"Oh, I thought you were upstairs." He pushed Lulu down, her front paws clicking against the wood floors.

Sensing her playtime was over for 24 hours, she ambled toward her bed in front of the fireplace and sat down.

I stood on the bottom step, shuffling my feet awkwardly like a middle schooler at a school dance.

"I'm headed out." He reached for his bag but hesitated as I remained on the stairs. I'm not typically one to struggle with a loss of words, so David probed deeper. "Are you okay? You seem weird. Did I forget someone's birthday?"

I managed to pry my arm loose from its position against my back. My hand shook as I held out the white stick with two little lines that would change our story forever.

There are so few moments in life when people are genuinely surprised. Even rarer are the surprises that bring pure joy. His eyes softened and his smile grew brighter than I ever remembered seeing it. His head tilted to one side as tears brimmed in his eyes. He wrapped his arms around my waist and nestled his head on my shoulder, while I still stood on the trusty stair. Then he cupped my face in his hands for a tender kiss. Tears mixed with giggles as we savored the news together. He reluctantly grabbed his bag and flashed a wide smile as he turned to leave.

"Remember to call your mom on your way. It's her birthday," I called as he stepped off the sidewalk and onto the driveway next to his truck, throwing his bag into the passenger seat.

"Got it." He turned with one more grin as he opened his door and looked back to where I stood at the edge of the sidewalk.   Lulu had followed me out, apparently curious about the sudden sea of emotion filling our normally quiet house. "And remember, we agreed not to tell anyone!" His door swung shut.

David: *In typical guy fashion, I assumed when Ashley said, "Don't tell anyone," she actually meant, "Don't tell anyone important, like our parents." I lasted about five minutes at the firehouse until I blurted out the news to my co-workers. Ashley looked shocked when she found out I had told the guys at work, but how could she be mad for long? It was such exciting news! I was going to be a dad! How could I keep that a complete secret?*

Mother's Day was just a few weeks away and I knew that would be the perfect setting to tell our parents that they would all be grandparents for the first time. Even though Mother's Day was less than two weeks away, it felt more like two years. I had never kept much of anything from my mom, especially not news like this! We attend church with my parents. I talk to my mom almost every day and see her frequently. My mom doesn't even knock when she comes to our house. She has a key and lets herself in. On more than one occasion David has stood at the top of the stairs and said, "Hey Ash, I guess your mom's here. She's standing in the living room." Our relationship made keeping news like a pregnancy under wraps difficult.

Mother's Day finally arrived. It doesn't take much to evoke emotions from our parents, especially my mom. I knew no matter how we told them, it would be a memorable, sweet time for them, but I wanted to make it unique, not just walk in and blurt out: "We're having a baby." I found a poem, typed it out and put it in two Mother's Day cards:

I do not have a face to see
or put inside a frame.
I do not have sweet cheeks to kiss,
I don't yet have a name.
You can't yet hold my tiny hands,
Nor whisper in my ear.
It's still too soon to sing a song
Or cuddle me so near.
But all will change come January,
That's when they say I'm due.
I'm your new grandbaby,
I can't wait 'til I meet you.
All I ask between now and then
Is patience as I grow.
I promise I'll be worth the wait,
Because of all the love we'll know.
So what I have to give you now,
Is a wish to you from me.
I cannot wait to be a part
Of this wonderful family.
-Baby Hallford

Sunday lunch at my grandmother's is a tradition on most holiday weekends. The smell of a southern, country feast still lingered in the air as we watched my mom open her card, shifting from side to side in our seats. Her face broke into a huge smile as tears began forming in the corners of her eyes. She rushed around the table, scooped me into her arms, and rocked me back and forth as she patted my back.

"A baby! Tommy, a baby! Can you believe it?" The words cascaded out through a stream of joyful tears. As she released her grip, she gasped, "Well, how long have you known?"

I'm not sure what shocked her more – that I was expecting a baby or that I had kept the secret from her for weeks! My dad quietly basked in the joy of the moment, leaning back in his chair and cupping his hands over his face. Laughter, tears of joy, and screams of excitement filled the air all afternoon. It was like releasing the pressure on a tightly fitted valve – relief!

Later that evening, we made the twenty-minute drive to my in-law's house. We could barely contain our excitement. David's dad, Richard, while typically quiet and reserved, has an incredibly tender heart. His tears were flowing alongside Patsy's at the news of a grandbaby.

David: *It's a pretty special thing to tell your parents you are going to have a baby. I had never really thought about it before, but seeing the delight on my parents' faces brought me a joy I didn't anticipate. Since this was before the days of making announcements "Facebook official," we took time to call my brother, Nathan, and his wife, Krista, to tell them the news. We arrived home later that night exhausted: church, two Mother's Day celebrations, and a baby announcement made for a full day.*

The pregnancy progressed beautifully. I felt guilty when other women talked about their struggles to get pregnant or the complications they experienced during pregnancy. Not me. I loved it. I loved the little flutter kicks I began to feel. I loved knowing this baby could hear my voice above anything else. I loved knowing my body was designed for this – to nurture a little baby from conception to birth. Apparently, I was a little too effusive about the wonders of what my body was accomplishing because David felt free to tease me anytime I did voice a complaint. He would say, "Man up, you were made for this! God didn't make everyone equipped to be barefoot and pregnant in the kitchen." The glint in his eye and quick smile would flash before he zipped around the corner, out of the range of me throwing a pillow at him. I dished out enough jokes that I knew I had to be able to take them too.

Before I knew it, the calendar had flipped to August. Georgia is hot – especially in August. The air is so thick, it sticks to your skin, the sun so relentless that no one enjoys being outside for anything other than a dip in the pool. In the air-conditioned kitchen, I impatiently tapped my spoon on the side of my bowl, the oatmeal drenched in butter and brown sugar stood still too hot to heat. I continued fidgeting with my spoon as I fought to suppress the anticipation that had been building for

14

months. Inside a bright red circle on the calendar read the words: Ultrasound 10:00AM. It didn't seem real that in just a few hours, we would know so much more about this little baby growing inside me.

David and Lulu bounded downstairs, Lulu heading straight for the backdoor. David poured a cup of coffee and grabbed a banana out of the bowl at the edge of the counter.

"You ready?" he asked, opening the door to let Lulu back in. She bolted in, panting ferociously from the oppressive heat already present at 9:00AM.

"I've been ready for about four months. Let's go," I replied as I left the remaining few bites of oatmeal in the bowl and placed it in the sink. I struggle to eat on a nervous stomach, so I was proud of myself for forcing anything down for breakfast that morning.

At 10:00 o'clock sharp, the ultrasound technician appeared in the doorway to call me back to the exam room. Her eyebrows lifted in surprise at the entourage that followed me down the hallway. Both sets of parents came along, not wanting to miss this exciting news. As I climbed onto the table, our parents filed around the tiny room, soon feeling like sardines in a tin can. I'm told that those who aren't from the Deep South might not understand this business of packing the ultrasound room with both sets of parents, but this was the first grandbaby for either side, and in the South, family is thicker than the humidity, and you just don't leave your parents out. Their joy was palpable.

Time crawled as the ultrasound tech silently performed the necessary scans and measurements. At times, I caught myself holding my breath in anticipation. Finally, the tech casually asked, "Do you have any other questions?"

"Well, yes," I fumbled, wondering if she was serious. "What are we having?"

We were ready to be excited either way – boy or girl – but the joy on David's face was impossible to hide when the ultrasound tech announced: "It's a boy!"

Thoughts of planes, trains, trucks and dinosaurs began swirling through my mind. There would be no stopping Mimi, Maw-maw, or Aunt Krista from rushing out to Carters and Target on a search for baby boy outfits. Overalls, button-up shirts in green and blue, tiny blue jeans, khakis, and cowboy boots would soon fill the nursery's closet. The grandpas just smiled with pride – maybe clutching their wallets a little tighter in anticipation of those shopping trips.

We climbed into the car, David and I bubbled back and forth in conversation about boy names, nursery décor, future baseball teams, and firefighter dreams. As I lifted my dark hair off my neck, which was now damp with sweat from the short walk to the car, my hand brushed along my right jaw line.

"Not again," I thought, annoyed that the joy of the day was briefly interrupted by a stubborn lymph node.

I had discovered it back in early March when my friend AngeLeah invited me on a shopping trip to help her pick out some baby furniture. She and her husband, Wes, were expecting their first child early that summer. I still remember the sticker shock as I walked around the showroom. Babies would be expensive one day!

As AngeLeah and I were driving home through relentless Atlanta traffic with brake lights flashing like lightning bugs on a warm summer night, I felt it for the first time. I'm not even sure how. Maybe I was brushing my hair back or wiping something off my face. On the right side, just below my jaw bone my hand caught a lump. It was about the size of a pea. I figured it had to be a swollen lymph node and cringed in exasperation. We had so much going on, and I didn't have time to be sick.

Weeks later, I hadn't even noticed that the anticipated sickness never came. However, I did make an unexpected trip to the Emergency Room. My head had been pounding all day. Light was excruciating. Pulling my sweatshirt over my eyes trying to block out the light, I clutched the door handle fighting to keep my head still as the car swayed.

The waiting room had only a few available seats, but the receptionist could immediately see my misery. Her pace quickened as she watched me writhe. Her assurance that they would get to me as soon as possible didn't help much as I sat in the stiff waiting-room chair. After a few names had been called, I hoped I would be next. Just then a girl staggered in, blood pouring down her face and splashing against her muddy softball uniform. As her cleats clinked down the hallway toward a room, I couldn't help but mutter, "Well, there goes my slot."

Finally, my turn came. The doctor ordered Toradol to help alleviate the pain. As the medicine began to kick in, my muscles relaxed. The debilitating pain lifted gradually from my skull. As relief began to wash over me, I sank into the worthless pillow on the table, pulled the blanket that the nurse had left at the foot of my bed over me and pressed my eyes closed.

Lying in the bed, curtain drawn, listening to the hustle and bustle of the ER activity, I recalled the swollen lymph node that was still noticeable even after a few weeks. From my dark cocoon, I followed the sound of the doctor's footsteps down the hallway, thankful when they stopped outside my curtain.

"Could you take a look at this lymph node? It's been swollen for a few weeks."

The doctor seemed almost annoyed at my additional request. The waiting room was packed, and they needed my bed. I was pleased with myself though for thinking to ask and saving myself the hassle of a doctor's appointment on another day. He examined the lump, his hands ice-cold and a little damp from having just washed them. He determined I had an infection in my salivary gland and prescribed me an antibiotic. I was thankful to have an answer and a treatment so hurriedly for what had become a lingering annoyance.

I never saw that doctor again. I can only imagine what he would say if he had had the chance to examine me just a few months later.

Chapter 3
Baby Cruisin'

"Children are an heritage of the Lord; and the fruit of the womb is his reward." Ps. 127:3

Over the next few months, the knot under my jawline would come and go, come and go. When I had finished the round of antibiotics from the ER, the knot receded and almost disappeared completely only to return a few weeks later. When it returned, it would fluctuate between the size of a pea and the size of a quarter.

In early May, just after finding out I was pregnant, I made an appointment with my ear, nose and throat (ENT) physician, Dr. Parks. I recounted the first time I noticed the knot and my story of the trip to the ER. I also mentioned a history of cancer on my dad's side of the family including my grandmother and two aunts who had each had cancer to include breast cancer, throat cancer, brain cancer, and lymphoma. No one wants to sound paranoid but, in truth, I was, just a bit.

During his exam, he pressed lightly on the knot, which was tender to the touch but not painful. He asked a few more questions and eventually reached the same diagnosis as the ER doctor – an infected salivary gland. While he did not seem flippant at all, he also did not seem concerned. He said it was nothing to worry about and prescribed another round of antibiotics.

This began a cycle that would last for the next seven months: knot swells, antibiotics given, knot goes away. I'm not even sure how many rounds of antibiotics I took that summer. My feelings of frustration mixed with uncertainty as the weeks went on, but one thing was consistent – no one else seemed concerned. The doctor at the ER in March certainly hadn't seemed concerned. My ENT felt confident it was an infected salivary gland. David wasn't worried at all. He trusted the doctor's assessment. I even mentioned it to my sister-in-law, Krista, who is a Pediatric Intensive Care Unit (PICU) nurse.

Krista: *Sometimes when answering the phone, I'm not sure whether to say "Nurse Krista" or just hello. Friends and family often call with various pains and aliments, wanting my medical advice to ease their minds. The situations always turned out to be minor or went away on their own, so when Ashley called late that summer, telling me about the knot in her neck, I didn't think much about it. The fact that it would go away and come back led me, and the staff I worked with, to believe that it was nothing serious. I assured her serious things, like cancerous tumors, don't just come and go.*

In late July, I saw my primary care doctor for an unrelated issue. During her exam, she noticed the knot, which seemed a little more swollen that day than it had been. I quickly recounted all of the doctor visits up to that point and the consistent diagnosis of an infected salivary gland. I also mentioned the family history of cancer, just to be thorough – not paranoid.

Her eyes narrowed, wrinkling her brow above her brown rimmed glasses.

"I want to send you for an ultrasound," she said as I sat up on the table, swinging my legs around the side to face her.

"This has been going on long enough that we need to take a closer look at what's going on. An ultrasound is not ideal. An MRI or CT would give us a better picture, but since you are pregnant, an ultrasound is the best option we have." I sensed a layer of concern beneath the matter of fact tone in her instructions.

The following week, I checked in for my ultrasound. It was disappointing to be having an ultrasound and not get to see my baby. Ultrasounds of the neck are not nearly as exciting. I settled onto the table, my belly not yet big enough to make lying on my back uncomfortable, but I regretted my decision to wear shorts. The dimly lit room felt considerably cooler than the air outside! I stared up at the gray ceiling tiles as the technician squeezed a dollop of warm gel on my neck. At times it was difficult to swallow as she pressed the wand along my jaw line to get a clear image. I prayed silently as she worked.

When she finished, she handed me a cloth to wipe the gel from my neck and cheek.

"How did everything look?"

"The radiologist will review the images and send the report to your doctor."

I sighed. I knew she was just doing her job, but I hoped for some small indication of whether or not everything looked normal. The next day, the doctor finally called.

"The radiologist feels certain it is just a swollen salivary gland. It seems my concern may have been unnecessary. You may have stones in the gland causing it to swell, which could easily be removed after you have the baby. If it continues to bother you after you deliver, follow up with me and we will get a CT scan for a better look," she concluded, her tone lighter than it had been before.

Despite the nuisance the knot had become, I felt at ease knowing it was nothing serious. Ironically, David's dad, Richard, was diagnosed with stones in his salivary gland shortly after my ultrasound. He had the stones removed with no complications. This helped further comfort me, seeing that it seemed like such a simple issue to correct.

David: *I'm not really one to go to the doctor. I pretty much have to be dying to go in, so I thought there may be some overreaction over the knot in Ashley's neck. I felt sure it was nothing serious, especially after my dad's diagnosis. Ashley still wanted answers though. She waffled between trusting the doctor's diagnosis and feeling like they were missing something. I was more worried that she had convinced herself that something was wrong than I was concerned that something actually was.*

At a follow up visit with Dr. Park, he still wanted to rule out any infection. Since we had no clear answers either way, it made sense to pursue both possibilities – infection or salivary gland stones. He referred me to an infectious disease doctor for a second opinion. The run of the mill antibiotics that I had been taking were clearly not working, and Dr. Parks hoped a more specialized doctor could pinpoint exactly what kind of infection we were dealing with and help chart a better course of treatment. The visit yielded little. He suggested a PICC (Peripherally Inserted Central Catheter) line for the stronger antibiotics he would prescribe. I wasn't sure exactly what a PICC line was, but it sounded basically like a do-it-yourself IV. No thanks. In the end, it was just another doctor and another round of stronger antibiotics, but unfortunately, with the same result.

I wanted to push the concern for the annoying knot far from my mind in early September. I had a vacation to plan. Babymoons have become a common practice – a trip before the birth of a child. These vacations are complete with uninterrupted sleep, no strollers or diapers bags, as the new parents exerting a last burst of freedom and spontaneity before schedules and sleepless nights become a way of life. The weeks hummed along as I bought my first maternity outfits and made preparations for the trip. Not only did we plan a babymoon, we decided to make it a family affair and invited our parents and my brother to join us.

We love cruises. David and I grew up going on cruises and we enjoyed going together during the early years of our marriage. For us they are the ideal vacation – the perfect mix of relaxation, activities, sight-seeing and of course, amazing food. Maybe I like them so well because everything is so carefully planned that my inner control freak can take a break for a week.

While both sets of our parents had grown from acquaintances when we were kids to casual friends when we were dating, this trip presented one of the first opportunities for them to spend an extended amount of time together. I often assumed our parents were closer friends than they actually were. David and I had first "met" when we were just five years old, and our childhoods were so similar, it was as if we were living parallel lives. If you ask David his first memory of me, inevitably he will talk about my lunchbox – an aqua-green and white lunchbox. In the cafeteria before school, he remembers that I would walk in, quickly slide into the seat at the far end of the table and slink behind my lunchbox. I guess that's why he remembers it so clearly – it was all he could see of me most mornings. If I had known that lunchbox would be such a pivotal part of my story, I may have put a little more thought into the selection process. (Baby Hallford would have to have a great lunchbox!)

Our families loaded the cars in late September for the seven-hour drive to St. Augustine, Florida, two days before our boat's scheduled departure. Our family can't seem to accomplish much without speed bumps of excitement! Love bugs (firefly-looking bugs that mate in swarms during the fall in the southeast) had plastered our car during the drive, and we needed to blast them off before they turned to cement. We found a hand painted "Free Car Wash" sign and against better judgment, pulled in.

After being instructed to pull around back, we were surprised to see the car wash consisted of a man and his young daughter, probably about eight years old, come out to wash the bugs off…by hand. The quality of the wash turned out to be exactly what you would expect, given the method, but we rolled our eyes and drove on. Little did we know, the remaining love bugs would eventually ruin the paint on my parents' car! So much for a "free" car wash.

That evening at the hotel, I started feeling what I thought were contractions. Completely clueless to all things labor and delivery, I assumed they were just Braxton Hicks contractions, not the real thing. I knew that there would be minimal medical care on a boat in the middle of the ocean if I went into labor early, so I tried to brush off the contractions and focus on the trip.

Sheila: Ashley mentioned the contractions to me that night, and I agreed with her that they were probably just her body's way of getting ready to have the baby. She brought us to her hotel room the night before the ship left

– that baby boy was kicking around like a roped calf and she wanted us to feel him move. As she laid back on the bed, her belly jostling back and forth, I noticed her rub her neck. She asked me and Patsy to feel it. While she was slightly concerned about the contractions, Patsy and I grew more concerned about the knot in her neck. I expected it to feel tender like a lymph node, but instead it felt more like a small Lego brick had been inserted below her jaw bone. Her doctors had assured her it was a salivary gland, and while I was no doctor, it sure didn't feel like a salivary gland to me. She didn't seem too worried about it though, so I tried to follow suit and enjoy our time as a family.

The next morning, we boarded and anticipated the fun of seven days and nights together on board the glistening ship. Since I was pregnant, the food looked and tasted more appealing than ever before. My favorite indulgence was a gooey caramel cake dripping with icing and crushed pecans. We enjoyed excursions, exploring the islands, and relaxing on the beaches. As I lounged on the sand one afternoon watching kids splashing nearby, I imagined how different our next vacation would be with children in tow!

Since, my feet were terribly swollen from the pregnancy and the heat, we tried to find activities that didn't include a lot of walking. When we docked at St. Thomas, we took a gondola up to Paradise Point. The view was breathtaking – the crystal blue water and the green hills dotted with pristine white houses. But, amidst the beautiful scenery all around me, I couldn't help focusing on all those gathered close to me: my husband, my parents, my brother, my in-laws, and the little guy spinning around in my tummy, (who we nicknamed BB, for Baby Boy, since we still hadn't decided on a name). I soaked in all the love that surrounded me like rays of sunshine. The warmth that filled my heart could not be eclipsed by any excursion or experience on the cruise.

Looking back, it is clear to see how the Lord knit our hearts closer together during that trip and how He meticulously orchestrated seemingly insignificant details for a divine purpose. Our parents grew not just as in-laws but also as friends. We all learned more about each other and grew closer as a family. We had no idea how valuable these strong family ties would become one day very soon.

Chapter 4
Old Souls

"I will bless the Lord at all times; his praise shall continually be in my mouth." Ps. 34:1

I drove to work on a crisp October morning still relishing memories of the cruise from two weeks before. The coolness of fall was just sweeping through the rolling, tree-covered hills of northwest Atlanta. The hot summer days were giving way to cool nights, football games, and pumpkin patches. I had graduated from Kennesaw State University with a degree in finance almost two years earlier, and I now spent my days working for a friend's collection agency. I enjoyed the variety of the work and developed an interest in legal affairs. I had even taken the LSAT in order to pursue law school before finding out earlier that year that I was expecting a baby.

I had just pulled the first file of the day to my desk when I felt a pain in my lower back. It subsided after a few seconds, and I thought it must be a muscle spasm. But then I felt it again. And again. Soon the pain, while not severe, wrapped around my torso. Since it was my first pregnancy, I didn't want to jump to the conclusion that I may be experiencing contractions, but after about an hour, the pain seemed too consistent to ignore. I couldn't imagine what else it could be.

I called my doctor's office and explained what was going on and felt relief when they wanted me to come in. I knew something wasn't right and had worried that my concern might be brushed off as nervousness of a first-time mom. I told my boss I needed to leave and called David on my way.

On the twenty-minute drive from my office to the doctor's, I focused on staying as calm as possible. I didn't know exactly what was happening, but I knew enough to know I needed to be calm for my baby. I took long, purposeful breaths, and I prayed. I wanted nothing more than a healthy pregnancy and a healthy baby. I had never really imagined anything else.

As I walked up to the office door, another contraction started. I paused, took a breath, and then walked into a crowed waiting room. The receptionist, busy on a phone call, gave me a slight wave and told me to have a seat after signing in. The chairs felt especially stiff that day, not at all what a pregnant woman would voluntarily sit in for any length of time. Thankfully, after just a few minutes, I heard my name.

"Ashley?"

I looked up.

"Come on back."

A midwife came through the door just a few minutes later. She examined me, and to her surprise, I was dilated to one centimeter at just 27 weeks. This was not good news. This was not following my carefully laid-out plan.

She prescribed complete bed rest. My mouth dropped open in disbelief. "Well, just my luck. I buy a maternity wardrobe and I end up on bed rest," I thought. I normally keep a pretty busy schedule, and it took me a few minutes to wrap my head around the idea of sitting at home for the next three months. It was not the type of decision I wanted to negotiate though – not with the health of my baby at stake. I knew he needed to stay put for at least ten more weeks, and I committed to doing everything in my power to help him stay there. After the midwife left, I walked down the short hallway to the front desk to set up my next appointment.

While bed rest would be devastating news to some, a small piece of me was excited. Despite the anxiety about experiencing pre-term labor, I looked forward to the quiet times at home that this would bring. I made a mental checklist of all the things I could accomplish – folding baby clothes, finishing thank-you notes, reading parenting magazines, and making lists of things we needed to do to decorate the nursery. With David's schedule at the fire department – one-day-on and two-days-off – he would be around several days a week to help take care of things around the house.

My couch served as home base for the foreseeable future. The close proximity to the kitchen made it easy for me to grab something to eat without exerting too much effort. Going upstairs to the bathroom was the most strenuous activity that faced me. I approached the stairs cautiously like a sloth on a tree.

"Stay in there, little boy," I urged BB with each methodical trip up the stairs.

I folded clothes and made to-do lists just like I had planned and probably watched one too many episodes of *House Hunters* during the day. At least with me at home more, Lulu couldn't get herself into any trouble.

"A baby should be a breeze compared to you," I chided after finding a pair of flip flops in shreds that morning.

As if learning to live with another human being isn't challenging enough, why is it that newlywed couples feel the need to bring an animal into the mix? Despite warnings from wiser family and friends, just weeks after getting married in 2004, David and I started looking for a dog. Not just a dog, but a puppy. We decided to look for a Jack Russell Terrier because David had that kind of dog growing up. David was smitten at first sight.

We were so naïve to pet ownership, despite having both had dogs growing up. Lulu got herself into all sorts of trouble early on – chewing on furniture, tearing shoes apart and just wreaking havoc in the house. We didn't put in the time and effort needed to house train a puppy well. We weren't even sure where to begin. We saw an advertisement for dog trainers that claimed to be able to house train a dog in a day, for the right price. Maybe Lulu wasn't a good student or we weren't good listeners, or maybe the trainers were scammers. We might as well have held our $500 up in the wind and let it blow away. They had us shake a set of chains to prompt Lulu to obey. We shook those chains for months, eventually feeling like idiots as she jumped around and continued with her naughty ways. With both of us working and me going to school at night, she was probably bored out of her mind. Looking back, we probably should have gotten two dogs, not one. Or, maybe none.

With me on best rest, David and I found it easy to continue the nightly routine we had developed since we first got married. We have always been what you would call old souls. We would cook something simple for dinner – sloppy joes, tacos, or burgers and then we would set up our trays in the living room. We settled in for our regular TV line up: *Everybody Loves Raymond, Seinfeld, Wheel of Fortune* and *Jeopardy*. We kept this routine up for years. Looking back, we acted more like a retired couple than young college kids! It was such a change of pace from the crazy schedule we kept most of the week between work, school, church, and family commitments. The calm predictability of those evenings enticed us home when we could have gone out. Now on bed rest, I longed for a little less old-soul routine, but I would do whatever it took to keep BB safe and sound in my belly for a few more weeks.

Just before the cruise we had ordered a new couch for our living room. It was delivered during my first week of baby house arrest. The timing couldn't have been better. When we were first married and just trying to scrape by financially, our house was furnished with a mixture of hand-me-downs and yard sale bargains. The only matching set of furniture we owned was our bedroom set. The light wood painted with flowers wasn't exactly what my firefighter-aspiring husband would have picked out. My parents had given it to me on my thirteenth birthday though, and with money tight, free furniture seemed to be our best option. We felt like actual grown-ups with a new couch!

As we were slowly replacing hand-me-down furniture with real purchases, I dreamed of the perfect nursery. Pottery Barn images filled my head, but I was on more of a Target budget. Registering for baby items had been way more fun than registering for pots and pans when we got married. Through showers and gifts, the décor for the little room began to come together. As I walked by the nursery one evening, I paused, noticing the boxes that had been piling up.

I took a step into the room and rubbed my belly as I closed my eyes, imagining a little boy in the neatly decorated room. I thought back to when we were discussing the decision to have kids just a year earlier. At the time, David and I were still wrestling with the decision faced by many young professionals: prioritizing career goals or family aspirations. Now, a year later, I couldn't have imagined our life another way. We had made the right decision.

Our January due date would come soon enough, and we would need to set aside time to tackle the nursery, making everything just right for our little boy. I wanted to be hands-on for that project, so the boxes and decorations would just have to wait until closer to my due date when I had a little more freedom to be up and about. The room went dark as I flipped the switch – we still had plenty of time.

Chapter 5
Biopsy au Natural

"Have I not commanded thee? Be strong and of good courage; be not afraid, neither be thou dismayed; for the Lord thy God is with thee whithersoever thou goest." Joshua 1:9

Monday, November 12, 2007

While most people were dreading the start of the work week, I felt a strange anticipation, a nervous energy. All the laundry was folded and put away, while every clean dish was in its place. The floors were swept and mopped and all the sheets were fresh. The house smelled like a Lysol commercial. While technically still on bed rest, my body refused to sit still. I worked as gingerly as I could, coaching BB on good cleaning techniques as I went.

David had just wrapped up an unusually quiet 24-hour shift at the firehouse. He lumbered down the stairs, pushing past Lulu toward the coffee pot.

"Can we leave a few minutes early," I asked, backing up against the counter and looking out the window to line of trees in the back yard. The vibrant yellow and orange hues of the oak leaves stood in sharp contrast to the myriad of pine trees lining the edge of the yard. "I need to run by the post office and bank on our way," I said, admitting to myself that I just wanted an excuse to get out of the house.

I put my coffee mug in the dishwasher as he shrugged in agreement and turned back to the stairs. Lulu bounced along behind him.

I wouldn't normally categorize myself as a hypochondriac, especially before the days of Google. I didn't typically research every symptom I had or get flustered by illness. However, this knot nagged me in a way I had never experienced before. I would waver between annoyance and concern: annoyance because I was pregnant and didn't want to take medication or add extra doctor visits and concern because of what everyone fears when they have a "knot" – cancer. After all, cancer had affected several women on my dad's side of our family. As the months wore on, knowing the family history, I found it harder and harder to brush it off entirely.

At the beginning of November, a few days after the latest cycle of antibiotics, the knot came back but this time with a vengeance. The brick-like density was accompanied with a throbbing pain, radiating down my neck. Shooting, searing pains layered over the throbbing made it impossible to ignore. Despite the clear ultrasound, Dr. Parks agreed to further testing. A biopsy was scheduled for the following week. We needed answers.

I wondered if I should be scared. Wouldn't a biopsy rattle most people? More than fear however, I felt an anxious anticipation. I was ready. Ready to know. Ready to know what really lay just under the surface of my skin. I was ready to face it head on. Or so I thought.

David: *Given my dad's recent diagnosis and treatment for stones in his salivary glands, I remained optimistic about Ashley's situation. I felt sure that once she delivered the baby, the doctors would be able to figure out what was going on and remove the stones, if necessary. Looking back, I think it may have been denial or somewhat willful ignorance. I try not to dwell on things that cannot be changed and not to worry over situations. However, I couldn't ignore the fact that she was about to have a biopsy. I had to admit to myself that doctors don't perform biopsies if there is absolutely no cause for concern.*

We had no idea what was waiting for us when we arrived at Kennestone Hospital, just north of Atlanta. David wound the car up the ramp of the parking garage. The rhythmic pat of our shoes on the ground was the only sound I could hear as we entered the walkway over the street below. I soon wished I had not worn a sweater. Even though the light November breeze felt cool, the air inside seemed stuffy, like they had just turned on the heat.

My stomach churned as we sat in the waiting room, basically rubbing elbows with other patients. We were lucky to find two seats together given the crowd that morning. My confidence morphed into worry. Due to the pregnancy, I wouldn't be able to have a local anesthetic during the procedure. For one that had never dealt well with pain, the anticipation was excruciating. The fear of possibly having cancer was overshadowed by the fear of the pain from the procedure. I tried to keep my mind off what was about to happen. I kept checking my watch as if I had somewhere else to be. Sweat began to collect on my hands.

I looked around the room and wondered what brought each person there. Inevitably bad news awaited a good portion of us. Statistics don't lie. Some of these people would die from the result waiting in their chart. Some would walk out with good news, like a bird soaring through the sky on a cloudless, breezy day. Our lives literally hung in the balance as we sat around flipping through magazines. The lady across from me munched mindlessly on a bag of popcorn. I almost gagged. I could never eat while I felt so nervous.

I rubbed my growing belly to calm my nerves. As I felt the baby kick and swirl in my belly, I watched a little boy across the room running back and forth. His mom wasn't having much success in keeping him entertained with crayons and paper. He wanted to climb chairs instead. The area around him was littered with cracker fragments, another vain attempt to keep him occupied. I wondered why she didn't just take her kid out of the room. Smugly I thought, "That will never be my kid," as most soon-to-be parents would say. Parenting was so easy from a distance.

David thumbed through a fishing magazine and occasionally glanced up at the news streaming on the TV. How could he be so calm? But then, he generally was the calmer one. Little did I know the anchor his calmness would become.

Finally, a nurse led us down the hall. Hospitals often feel like a labyrinth of hallways only navigable by a nurse that knows the way. After our series of turns, she led us into a room where they did blood work. In the back corner stood another doorway leading to a small room where they performed the biopsies. I was already so nervous, and yet my nervousness seemed to be increasing exponentially by the minute. My hands were shaking, and I felt sick to my stomach. Fear of pain, loss of control, and fear of the unknown were like a thick blanket enveloping me. My head and body were already swirling before I ever reached the table. I thought the panic might overtake me before they even had a chance to get started.

I laid down on the kid-sized table and immediately felt nauseous. My 32-week pregnant belly pushed all my organs up to my throat. I tried to adjust my lower body in a way that would bring at least some relief from the discomfort. Moving around while pregnant made me feel like a beached whale, especially while trying to navigate a tiny table. I shifted and pushed until I found a position that was bearable. In a few moments, the discomfort of pregnancy would be the last thing on my mind.

When the doctor came in, he marched over to the row of instruments lining the table, examining each one briefly before snapping on his gloves. I suppose a biopsy is not the time for small talk and pleasantries. Needles were prepped, vials made ready, and slides smeared. The nurse scurried back and forth at the doctor's request, finishing the preparations.

"I will insert four needles into four different regions of the mass and remove small pieces each time," he explained from behind his mask. "Due to your pregnancy, we won't be able to use any anesthetic. Just try to stay as still as possible and I will work as quickly as I can."

Sixteen sticks seemed manageable until the first one.

No amount of mental planning prepared me for the pain of the first needle. It was excruciating. Compounding the pain of the first needle stick was the knowledge of fifteen more to follow.

After the first four sticks, I was about to come off of the table, my huge baby belly and all. Again and again and again. Feeling frantic, I sobbed uncontrollably, shaking, dizzy, and sick. Despite the pain, I tried desperately to keep my body still. While needles pierce your neck, it is not the time to flail around like a fish.

David: *The biopsy was horrific to watch. I wasn't even allowed to stand next to her during the procedure. From across the room, I felt completely helpless. Watching my wife and unborn son go through such an ordeal was almost more than I could bear, even as a firefighter and EMT. I wanted to take her place, do anything to ease her suffering in that moment. Tears stung my eyes with every needle.*

The nurses and the doctors worked quietly and quickly, knowing the tremendous pain this was causing. To inflict that much pain on a pregnant woman must have been heart wrenching for even a trauma-hardened medical team. I cannot imagine what the doctor was thinking as he had to repeatedly stick me. After all, he was sure that this was nothing to be concerned about, but he needed the biopsy to see what kind of infection we were dealing with.

At last, it was over. Unfortunately, there was little relief. The mass in my neck was throbbing so badly, I didn't know if I could even stand up. I felt like I needed further attention after my ordeal, but no one seemed to notice. As I lay there, I could hear the medical team talking. The doctor and nurse must have been amazed at what he had extracted. I could hear them saying, "Oh, that is a good one…it's so grainy…Oh, this one is perfect…" I don't know if they thought I couldn't hear them because I was so traumatized or if they just didn't care. I just wanted to go home. Although time seemed to freeze during the procedure, it immediately went into fast forward. I was expected to get up and walk out as if nothing had happened.

Eventually the pain subsided. My eyes began to focus, and I wiped the tears from my cheeks. David slid his arm under my shoulders and helped me slowly sit up. I imagined make-up smeared across my face and hoped we wouldn't pass anyone we knew on the way out. The doctor had been out of the room for several minutes before I felt strong enough to stand up. Steadying myself on David's arm, I pressed my feet onto the floor. I would have taken a wheelchair to the car if one had been offered. We finally managed to navigate the maze of hallways and cross the walkway back to our Honda CRV.

I called my mom on the drive home and recounted the dreadful ordeal. She tried valiantly but she couldn't mask the concern in her voice as she assured me everything would be okay. I walked into the house and collapsed on the couch. At the time, it was the worst pain I had ever experienced, and I thought it would be the worst thing I would ever go through.

I sat by the phone all afternoon. My doctor had told me he would receive the report from the doctor who performed the biopsy and let me know as soon as he could. By evening, the phone was still silent. An already taxing day dragged on and on. Not only were David and I on edge, so was our family. My mom called for an update. David's mom called. My sister-in-law, Krista wanted an update as well.

Finally, late in the evening, the doctor called. I think I answered before the first ring had finished. I expected him to say they had determined the type of infection, call in a new prescription and that would be it. Instead, he began to tell me that the doctor who performed the biopsy had been reviewing the slides all afternoon. He went on to say that he couldn't tell what it was and was going to wait and get a second opinion the following day. My heart sank and a new level of fear set in. Why couldn't they tell what it was? What did that mean?

I tossed and turned endlessly, despite being physically exhausted. My mind went through the two possible scenarios over and over and over again. Either I had one of the weirdest infections they had ever seen or it was cancer. Maybe it was the kind of stones Richard had had a few months before. Those were the only options, right? If they knew for sure it wasn't cancer, then why didn't they at least tell me that over the phone so I wouldn't worry all night?

The next morning, I tried to rest. The trauma of the previous day had been enormously draining. I knew I needed to recover. I was having some contractions, and my immediate instinct was to protect my baby. I rested on our couch all morning while the TV was on, but it was just like white noise to my whirling thoughts. How did I even get to this place? I was normally a happy, carefree person. It was like a switch had flipped and now I was a crazy person obsessed with the idea that I had cancer. Doctor after doctor had assured me that there was no need for concern. My ultrasound had been clear. Despite my best efforts, I couldn't bring my thoughts to a manageable place. I tried to pray, but my thoughts were easily distracted. I needed answers and I needed them now!

David, on the other hand, had no doubt that it was an infection. He speculated that it was an infection that was typically treated with medication that could not be prescribed to someone while they were pregnant and that the delay was simply the doctors trying to come up with a strategy. He was not ignoring the worst-case scenario. He was just firmly on the other side...at least outwardly. Or maybe he refused to believe anything could be wrong because he didn't want anything to mess up his hunting trip!

David: *I had planned to go hunting for the evening. I would only be twenty minutes down the road in the woods behind my parents' house. I grew up going hunting. The woods were my solace. I hesitated to keep my plans after the events of the last two days, but Ashley encouraged me to go. I worried about leaving her, seeing her so anxious, but she assured me she was fine and that her mom was not far if she needed anything. I only agreed to go because I truly did not expect the call to come before I got back. Knowing how busy doctors are, I thought it would be the next day before Dr. Parks called back with any further information, and Ashley was beginning to think the same thing.*

As I watched David leave that afternoon, I never dreamed that would be the last time I would be alone for years. If I knew it, I would have done something other than sit on the couch holding the phone.

Chapter 6
Cancer Lumps

"Fear thou not: for I am with thee: be not dismayed; for I am thy God; I will strengthen thee; yea, I will help thee; yea, I will uphold thee with the right hand of my righteousness." Is. 41:10

While I sat on the couch alone that afternoon, waiting for the phone to ring, Lulu sat at my feet flapping her tail on the hardwood floor.   Lulu wasn't typically known for being a calm dog, yet she refused to leave my side. Maybe she sensed the tension that filled the house and felt the need to stay close. My phone was tied to me like her leash around my hand. I closed my eyes, willing myself to get some sleep but without success. The baby, on the other hand, apparently did not need rest. He kicked my ribs like they were soccer balls. I shifted endlessly on the couch, trying to find a comfortable position to handle his swift movements.

"Harley, give momma a break, son," I scolded as I rubbed my sore ribs with my right hand, my gray lounge pants bunched up around my ankles.

Just a few weeks before, we had finally decided on his name – Harley Thomas. Since the ultrasound in August, we had tossed names back and forth. David routinely threw out ideas like Amos and Beauregard with a mischievous grin and then wondered why I questioned whether or not he could take the conversation seriously. I first suggested Harley Thomas (our Dads' names), and over time the name grew on us. I for one was thankful that Beauregard Hallford would not appear on a limb of our family tree.

Eventually Harley settled down from his latest rounds of somersaults, and I felt a wave of loneliness. At least when he moved around, I felt his presence as a comfort. My nerves were shot. I had tried and failed to distract myself all day. I was still technically on bed rest, although the day before had been anything but restful. I wanted to work on the nursery, but knew I should take it easy. I flipped through channels on TV until I just couldn't do it anymore. I shifted the remote restlessly in my hand. Then it finally happened.

Three times that day I had jumped to answer the phone, only to realize it wasn't actually ringing. But this time it was. And the news on the other end would change my life.

"Hello?"

"Hey, Ashley? It's Dr. Parks. Is David with you?"

My heart dropped. I didn't want him to go any further. I knew. No one asks if your husband is around when they are going to give you good news. My chest felt tight and I was suddenly dizzy.

"….the mass is malignant."

It felt like I had been dropped onto a high-speed train and stood watching my life fly by outside the windows. I didn't know what to do. I struggled to stay coherent. Although the call was brief, I'm sure he gave me more information than I can remember. So many things were going through my mind. I snapped back to reality long enough to catch Dr. Parks before the conversation ended. I said the only thing I could think to say.

"Am I going to die?"

"No, Ashley. We will not let you die."

And then I was alone. I dropped the phone, and I sat motionless in complete silence, void of any thoughts or emotions for a brief moment. And then, as if someone took an enormous sledge hammer to an already crippled dam, everything burst forth. Anger. Sadness. Outrage. Fear. Terror. Guilt. Grief. Uncertainty. Panic. Sadness. So much sadness. It all burst out of me in a way I had never experienced before. Being alone, I could feel the depths of this news on my own. No one could watch me or judge my response. I didn't have to temper my reaction, trying to hold my emotions back for the sake of those around me. To the depths of my soul, I let the news engulf me.

I cried. I tried to pray. I fought to bring my thoughts into focus. My prayers ended up simply being, "Please God," rather than full prayers. I had never really experienced any significant difficulty or trial in my life. I'm not sure I even knew how to pray. I had grown up in church my whole life. I knew the mechanics of prayer, sure. I knew it was on the list of things that Christians were supposed to do, but suddenly hit with such a wall of fear and uncertainty, the shifting sands of my meager prayer life quickly slipped away. I was reduced to crying, moaning, and begging God.

I felt sure hours had elapsed in this state, but as I came out of the thick brain fog, I glanced at the clock. To my complete shock, only minutes had passed. I gained enough composure to pick up the phone and frantically dial David's number. He didn't answer. I kept calling but got no answer. For a moment I wondered why he wouldn't be answering, but then I remembered he went hunting. He might not be out of the woods for a few more hours.

I was reeling. I wanted to talk to David. I wanted him home. I wanted him to tell me it would be okay. I needed his steadiness, his comfort, and his no-nonsense, no-worry outlook on the situation. I needed him to pray. I needed him to carry me through this storm.

Instinctively, I rubbed my stomach through all of this. I guess subconsciously I tried to comfort Harley during the midst of my incredible turmoil. Studies say that babies can pick up on a mom's emotions, even in utero. If so, poor Harley's world was being rocked. I had no idea what to expect in the coming days, but I knew I wanted to protect my son. In that moment, all I could do was rub my stomach and tell him it would be okay.

Between attempts to reach David, I called my parents. My mom answered before I realized it had started ringing. She had been anxiously awaiting any news.

"They said it's cancer," I blurted out.

"I'm on my way."

In that moment, I didn't even realize the weight my words had on those around me. Obviously, the diagnosis was devastating to me, but it was also devastating to my friends and family. I had no time to process the grief I had just unloaded on my own mother. Her daughter, carrying her first grandbaby, had cancer. Someone she had carried, just as I was carrying Harley, and nurtured through every milestone was now in the fight of her life. I had tunnel vision though. I couldn't process my own grief, much less help process others. I just wanted to talk to David.

Sheila: As Tommy drove to their house, I just wept and prayed, thankful I didn't have to drive. Ashley's brother Joshua sat in the back seat as we all drove along in stunned silence. When my kids were little and would fall and get a boo-boo, they would come to me and point to where it hurt, and I would work my magic. When they were scared, I would pull them up close to me and whisper that everything would be all right. What can I say now? What do I tell my daughter that has just been diagnosed with cancer? How do I make things better? I'm her mom. I'm supposed to make everything better, but I can't. I have no magic this time. This is something only God can kiss and make better. I wanted to be her rock, but I knew I couldn't. There was no way I could get her through this on my own, and I was so thankful I didn't have to.

I couldn't sit still. I called AngeLeah. I gave her what little news I had. Just then, my parents and my brother rushed in. They never knock at my door and under the circumstances, they weren't about to start. My mom's face was red and blotchy. My dad held a white handkerchief between his hands while my brother tilted his head underneath his hat. It was obvious they had been crying and were trying to maintain their composure as they walked through the door.

My phone buzzed before I could say anything to my parents. Before the first ring finished I answered, forcing the words out before David had a chance to say hello.

"He said it's cancer."

"What?? Is he sure?"

"I don't know. I don't know anything," I heard myself say. My mom buried her head in her hands as she sat down on the far edge of the couch.

Although I couldn't see them, I could hear David's tears and tell he was fighting hard to keep his voice steady.

"Okay, it's okay. It's going to be okay, Ash."

"Just come home," I sobbed, tossing the phone on the couch before a wave of emotions crashed against me again.

David: *I had walked in the door to my parents' house and reached for my phone. Twelve missed calls. My heart sank. My parents knew as soon as my conversation with Ashley began. They could see the shock and concern on my*

51

face. I was already walking to my truck as I hung up the phone. I said, "She's got cancer," as I walked out. In that moment I couldn't think about how to break the news gently. I just reacted. I needed to get to my wife.

Not being there for Ashley in that moment is one of the biggest regrets of my life. I shouldn't have been in the woods. I should have been next to her. I felt selfish for going hunting, even though she told me it was fine. I should have known. She should never have had to receive that news on her own. I just didn't think the call would come that quickly and I certainly didn't dream that it would be bad news. I wavered between denial, disbelief, shock, and extreme concern. I couldn't wrap my head around the fact that my pregnant wife had cancer. I had a million questions. What would be the course of treatment? What would happen to Harley? How bad was it? Would she be okay?

The evening was a total blur. Our living room began filling with people: David, my parents, my brother, David's parents. Voices filled the rooms with questions hurled at me. I couldn't formulate coherent answers. I began to learn a lesson all cancer patients have to learn – the patient is usually the comforter in the family. You are the one who holds all the pieces, and if you crumble, so does everyone else. I would cry, and everyone else would cry, but then when I would pull it together, everyone else tried to as well.

I had so little information. One thing remained certain though – I would do everything in my power to protect my son. His well-being was my top priority. I couldn't entertain any course of treatment that would put him at risk. Being only 32 weeks along, I knew he needed more time. I resolved that I would do whatever it took to give that to him.

Wednesday, November 14, 2007

Ring. Ring. Ring.

I opened my eyes slowly at first, rolled to my side and pushed myself up. Had it been a dream? My hand instinctively went to my belly. I was still pregnant. Then my hand found the knot on my neck. Still there. Instantly the events of the previous day came flooding back. I had cancer. David stirred, jarring me from my thoughts.

Ring. Ring.

I snatched the phone, afraid it would stop ringing before I could answer, but I trembled at the thought of more bad news.

"Ashley? Its Dr. Soundararajan."

It was my OB. She talked 90 miles per hour. Dr. Soundararajan is a fiery lady who packs a huge personality into an 85-pound frame. She works and talks excessively fast; she is like a shot of espresso when you are already on a caffeine high. She is as sweet as they come but completely no-nonsense when it comes to the business of bringing babies into the world.

It was 7:00 AM. I had cried myself to sleep in David's arms. Having less than twelve hours to process the news that I had cancer, we were now being hit with a freight train of information. Not only was my doctor apparently caught up to speed on my condition, it seemed clear that she and my other doctors had an entire treatment plan mapped out.

"We have you setup for steroid shots this afternoon. You will need to get a couple of those before Friday. We have you scheduled for a tour of the NICU and an ultrasound to check on the baby before Saturday. We have your first appointment with your oncologist tomorrow. Your induction is set up for Saturday morning, so we will need to bring you in on Friday night to get that set up..."

I processed about ten percent of her words until I heard the word "induction."

"Wait, what...? My... my *what* Saturday morning?" I stuttered, flinging myself into an upright position as quickly and gracefully as possible at 32-weeks pregnant. I swung my legs around, hanging them off the end of the bed, revealing my white striped pajama pants and bare feet. David rubbed his eyes as he sat up behind me. A quick heel in the leg had helped bring him into the conversation.

"Your induction, Saturday morning," she repeated, clearly eager to move on with her instructions. I, however, was stuck on that point.

"What? Why??" Sure that I heard correctly, I was now standing up and pounding my heel into the floor as if my carpet was the object of my frustration.

"Yes, your ENT and I feel that it would be too risky to continue the pregnancy any further given your condition."

Her matter-of-fact tone let me know that apparently, this wasn't up for negotiation. I, however, had a different plan. I'm not exactly known for going with the flow. I'm rarely without a plan in any given situation. I certainly had a plan for this pregnancy, and voluntarily delivering a baby at 33 weeks did not fit that plan. Cancer would just have to wait.

"That's not a possibility. He's not ready. It's too early," I said with motherly authority.

"Ashley, you don't have a choice. Just be at the hospital this afternoon at 2:00. We are going to take him on Saturday, and he's going to be fine." Our heels continued to dig in further to our respective positions as the discussion continued.

My priority was my baby's life. I felt like her only priority was my life.

"This is absurd," I thought to myself as she persisted. "This baby is not ready. He just can't come before 37 weeks."

"Ashley, we can care for a baby that's a few weeks early. We cannot do anything for you while you are pregnant. He will be okay. I want to be able to say the same for you." The finality in her tone rang through the phone like the final chime on the stroke of midnight.

I had lost.

We hung up.

My heart felt broken. Cancer was bad enough, but now my baby would also be taken far too soon. I went from being on bed rest – doing everything in my power to keep this baby inside – to an induction – a forced evacuation seven weeks too early. This simply couldn't be happening. This wasn't the way it was supposed to happen.

Gasping for air between sobs, I crawled back onto the bed, collapsing in a heap among the pillows and blankets. I tried to relay the information to David, but it probably came out as a jumbled mess of facts between my tears and frustration.

David: *As she sputtered out bits of information to me, I realized how quickly this situation was spinning outside our control. I thought I had two more months to prepare to be a dad. I knew that no amount of time would prepare me for it totally, but I wanted to at least try. Nothing in the nursery was ready. That was my fault. As I sat in the bed, watching my wife break down in sobs, I felt utterly helpless. Everything was outside of my control and way beyond my knowledge or expertise. I wanted to do what was best for Harley and yet at the same time, what was best for Ashley. All I knew to do was trust the doctors.*

I did manage to write down the appointment times, so we started there. Our calendars as we knew them were wiped clean. Appointments, blood draws, and paperwork would come in rapid-fire succession. The first few days as a cancer patient are like trying to drink out of a firehose under the best of circumstances. Coupled with getting ready for a new baby seven weeks sooner than we had planned felt like drinking out of the firehose blindfolded.

Soon the phone rang again.

"Hey Ashley, it's Dr. Parks." His empathy felt palpable even over the phone. "I need to go over the details of the surgery to remove the tumor…"

This time I at least grabbed a pen and paper from my nightstand to take down the information he gave me. There were so many appointments that it was hard to keep them all straight. David appreciated the gesture at organization. We couldn't continue the pattern of him deciphering medical information through a torrent of sobs. Breaking down every five minutes wasn't going to help anyone. I took a deep breath, prayed, asked the Lord for strength, and fought to focus my attention on Dr. Park's instructions.

As I put down the phone and my pad of paper filled with instructions and appointment times, the vortex of uncertainty ramped up. Everything spun around me, far outside my reach of control. I grasped for anything that I could manage. I couldn't think about inductions and surgery and cancer treatments. I had to pick something, anything that I could control. I glanced at my closet. I stood up and marched over, determined to not sink completely into the mire of despair. Things as simple as what I would wear or what I would eat – I could determine that. I could control that, so I focused on that. Only a few hours into this ordeal and I ached for normal, for control.

David and I hurried to get dressed and get out the door. Our first stop was the ENT's office to complete all the pre-op forms and bloodwork for the surgery. I asked the nurse when the surgery would be scheduled. She could not give me an exact date but knew it would be soon after I delivered Harley. Once we were done there, we grabbed a quick bite of lunch, still unable to wrap our heads around all that had happened.

Later that afternoon, we arrived at the hospital and started down the list of tasks we needed to complete as if we were on a conveyer belt in an assembly line, moving from one station to the next. First, I had reams of paperwork to fill out for the induction that I didn't even want. Next, I went in for a steroid shot that would hopefully help Harley's lungs develop more quickly, followed by an ultrasound to check Harley's size and development.

After the ultrasound, we rode the elevator up to the Neonatal Intensive Care Unit (NICU), my navy-striped tunic hugging my baby bump. I realized all the maternity clothes I had been so excited to purchase would hardly be used. Between bed rest and delivering early, the clothes seemed like such a waste. I just added it to the list of things that didn't go according to my plan.

We were met at the door of the NICU by an older nurse whose name tag read Betty. She walked us through the lengthy procedure to sign in and wash our hands before entering the floor. After we were thoroughly scrubbed free of germs, she led us to the nurses' station in the center of the hallway. A group of doctors and nurses stood in a semi-circle ready to introduce themselves. After quick introductions, each one filed off, back to their respective work, until just one nurse remained. She guided us to a large room divided into six smaller areas by curtains where the hush was only broken with whispers and beeps of monitors. Her white shoes moved silently across the floor as she led us to the first curtain, pulling it slightly to one side. Situated in the center of the tiny room, stood a single isolette, holding a tiny, perfect little human attached to multiple cords and monitors.

"This is about the size of a 32-week-old baby to give you some perspective on what to expect," she explained, tugging the curtain back to its original position.

She led us to a small room directly across the hall. I reached for David's hand as she walked us through the basics of NICU care and prepared us for the long hospital stay Harley may endure.

"You need to be prepared for him to be whisked away to the NICU immediately after delivery. He probably won't be able to breathe on his own and will need breathing support."

I cringed. That's not at all what I had pictured when I dreamed of having my first baby.

She continued, "He probably won't cry at first, but don't be alarmed, that's normal."

The word "normal" struck me as terribly misplaced in this situation. Absolutely nothing in our world was normal. Nothing.

Lastly, she walked us around the corner to a cluster of doors, each one a small room with a bed, a chair, and a small round table. When Harley was ready to be released from the NICU, the nurse explained that we would have to stay overnight in one of these rooms before being released to go home. The staff needed to see a dry run in order to make sure we would manage everything on our own.

David: *The NICU was overwhelming. The procedures, the tiny, fragile babies, the somberness. On top of all that, the thought of our son not breathing on his own when he came into the world felt surreal. Ashley and I didn't even have time to process anything together. We were just being thrown information by the truck load and forced to deal with it as it came, with zero privacy and at warp speed. Ashley wanted me to go with Harley when he was taken the NICU. While I consented, I didn't want to think about any of it. The thought of my wife being separated from her son on top of everything else just seemed like pouring salt in her wound. Even though it was my child and my wife, I felt like a spectator, like I was being walked through a rehearsal of what was going to happen, feeling helpless to ease the pain of the two people most precious to me.*

Every stop we made in the hospital brought new rounds of emotions, but the NICU struck a deep chord of sadness and despair for me. I had carried this precious baby for almost eight months. I wanted nothing more than to see his sweet face and hug him, and yet everyone around me told me that, most likely, I wouldn't even get to touch him before they took him upstairs for treatment. I just kept crying, the emotions too intense to contain. I had no idea what it felt like to cuddle my own baby or to feed him and press him close. Thinking about any scenario other than holding him right away seemed too cruel to consider as a real possibility.

As we left the hospital that afternoon, I felt numb, as if I had been in a bumper car all day being slammed against a wall repeatedly. Overcome by the amount of information, I couldn't focus on even the smallest things. I knew there was so much I needed to do, but feeling so overwhelmed, I struggled to know where to start. I just sat on the couch, staring at the fireplace, unable to meld my thoughts into cohesive actions. I realized that I would be having a baby on Saturday – a tiny baby. Boxes littered the unfinished nursery with items needing assembly: the crib, the glider, the changing table. I had plenty of newborn clothes but nothing that would fit a tiny premature baby.

Just as I felt a fresh wave of panic, my mom suggested we go shopping to pick up some preemie outfits and grab other odds and ends that we may need for Harley's delivery. Someone suggested I buy a couple outfits from Build-a-Bear workshop. I laughed at first, until I realized my friend wasn't kidding.

"My friend's baby was so small that preemie clothes wouldn't even fit. If you want him in something other than a diaper, it may be your only option," she said.

Leaving the mall with stuffed-animal outfits along with some preemie clothes seemed laughable, but at least we were ready. I had something I knew my baby could wear, no matter how small he was. I welcomed the distraction of shopping with my mom after the whirlwind day we had had. Retail therapy is always fun, but especially when you are buying baby clothes. It brought a little ray of sunshine into an otherwise very dark cloud that began to envelope us.

Chapter 7
Nursery Night

"Bear ye one another's burdens, and so fulfil the law of Christ." Galatians 6:2

Thursday, November 15, 2007

I opened my eyes, blinking back the sunshine streaming through the cracks in the blinds. It was as if my life was on a cruel repeat in which I woke up, remembered I had cancer, and headed into a day filled with appointments. As I brushed my teeth, I started thinking of my other 26-year-old friends who were busy thinking about new careers, weddings, and the best brands of car seats while I was thinking about what my oncologist was going to say to me today. It felt surreal.

When I walked downstairs, David paced in front of the kitchen counter, his phone pressed to his ear. Two years earlier, he had accepted his dream job as a firefighter in the Cobb County Fire Department, one of the largest in Metro Atlanta. His dad had retired after 30 years serving in the same fire department. David had also taken classes at Kennesaw State and worked part-time at the Post Office when we got married, but his heart was always set on following in his dad's footsteps. During his rookie year at the station, he habitually received the brunt of good-natured jokes about how young he looked.

The other guys would often say he was the Lieutenant's son and it was "bring your kid to work day." He took the teasing easily and simply enjoyed every shift.

Now he was scrambling to rearrange his schedule to be with me as we prepared for Harley's birth and the surgery to remove the tumor. I assumed a co-worker had returned his call about switching his schedule for the weekend. (His fellow firefighters graciously agreed to switch schedules, donate their vacation, and work David's shifts throughout the next several months.)

When the call was over, we made the fifteen-minute drive down the winding backroads to the site of a brand-new hospital in our county. The physician building had just been completed. As we pulled in, even the lines on the parking lot were stark white against the black asphalt. The brilliant blue sky reflected off the mirrored windows as our entourage made its way inside – David and I, my parents, and his parents. When David opened the door into the office, I felt an unexpected sense of calm. I gazed around me at the beautiful space. It felt more as if we were waiting for a massage or a facial at a spa than to see an oncologist. The room even smelled new. I settled into a soft, oversized chair next to a floral lamp shedding soft light around me. The tranquility of the room calmed my nerves and made me feel safe despite the circumstances I faced.

We stopped by the lab before seeing the doctor. The tech drew vial after vial of blood. I lost count and just prayed I wouldn't pass out. After the lab, we were taken to a tiny exam room with the same spa-like décor and feel of the waiting room, but the size was certainly not designed for the crowd of people we attempted to squeeze into it.

You could cut the nervous energy with a knife. Finally, Dr. Miller walked in; I think she seemed more than a little surprised at the crowd of people waiting. She looked beautiful and sweet – not at all what I had expected. Her long blonde hair fell against her small frame, which was supported by three-inch black heels. Her white coat opened neatly over her blue and coral blouse and black pencil skirt. I'm not sure exactly what I pictured an oncologist to be, but she wasn't it--a pleasant surprise. Without her speaking a word, I trusted that she would get us through this.

"The first step will be to determine what kind of cancer you have," she began, her voice calm and steady, as if walking us through the halls on our first day of high school. "Once we know what we are fighting, I will be able to put a treatment plan together."

She scanned the room, making eye contact with each person, aware of the burden each one carried. "I will do my best for you and your family, Ashley," she assured me as her eyes came back to rest on mine. "However, one thing I want you to know – your journey lies in the hands of someone far more powerful than me. We just have to trust Him with the outcome."

In that moment, we didn't have answers and didn't even know the questions we should have asked, but we felt confident knowing that Dr. Miller shared our belief that God was in control.

Remarkably, I felt strangely calm until my very last question which had been persistently on my mind since the cancer diagnosis.

"Will I be able to have more children after chemotherapy?"

Her answer was one that I'll never forget. "Honestly, most of the time after chemotherapy, it is not possible to have another child. I can't say that for certain since we don't have an exact treatment plan yet, but I would say it is highly possible that you will never be able to carry another child."

I had kept it together pretty well until that revelation. I began to sob; my shoulders shook with the deep sadness flowing out of my heart. We had discussed me dying, and I took the news in with little reaction. We had discussed surgery and radiation and chemotherapy, and I held it together. However, the thought of not being able to have another child stretched beyond what I could comprehend. I didn't want to comprehend it. Dr. Miller came around the desk and put her arm around me.

"Aw, honey, it will be okay. Right now let's just be thankful for the child that you *are* carrying. He will help you through this probably more than you can imagine. He's going to be fine, and we are going to take good care of you."

In that moment, it didn't feel like enough. While I thanked the Lord for Harley, I knew I wanted more kids.

The desire went deeper than I could even express in words. Desperate, I asked, "Well what about harvesting my eggs? Couldn't we do that before the treatments start?"

Her brow furrowed under the wisp of blonde hair resting on her forehead.

"The most important thing for you right now is to start treatments as soon as possible. Fertility treatments would only delay that process. With cancer, time is never on our side."

Her voice, pleasant but firm, seemingly drew a line in the sand.

"Your tumor presented atypically during your pregnancy, suggesting it was possibly driven by hormones. Ashley, the same substance that would be used to stimulate your ovaries during fertility treatments would possibly be the precise fuel the cancer thrived on. Any cancer cells left in your body could spread rapidly. That is simply not a risk you should take."

My fist tightened as I moved from sadness to anger. I felt robbed. This hurt reached deep into my soul and struck at the core of who I was – a woman. My body was designed by God to have babies. I *wanted* more children. Why was this happening? I could not close the door on my dream of future children. I knew in my mind that the decision was not over, but for the moment, I had to move on.

After leaving Dr. Miller's office, we returned to the other hospital for the last steroid shot before Harley's delivery. At last, David and I drove home in silence. For the first time that day, we were alone. I sunk into the seat, thankful to not have to put on a brave face or answer any more questions. Small pockets of time when we could be silent or cry or vent all the frustrations of the day were a welcomed relief.

I pushed myself back up in the seat, forcing the self-pity from my posture. I couldn't do anything about future babies right then, but I could do something for the baby I was about to have: get the nursery ready for Harley to come home. Our procrastination had caught up with us. The nursery, still filled with boxes, needed a lot of work.

Strangely enough, my cancer diagnosis had brought me a new-found freedom. I had been on bed rest for weeks and now, suddenly, I could be up and about doing things I needed to do. I resigned myself to the fact that we could not get it all done the way I had hoped in just two days, but we could at least get the crib together and move some of the boxes out of the way. My planning was interrupted by my phone ringing.

Before the phone reached my ear, I heard my mom talking. She began rattling off plans for the night. I stopped her and told her to back up and start again. Maybe my mind was full of too many things, but I felt like everyone around me spoke at warp speed.

"We have it all arranged," she announced. "Tonight is 'Make the Nursery Happen Night.' Tons of people from church are on their way. We are going to get this done for y'all," she giggled as she relayed the details.

Sheila: Small churches are like family. People pull together to help and support in ways normally only family would. We attended Happy Valley Baptist Church with Ashley and David, a small church in a rural town on the west side of Atlanta. It was a brick church nestled in a fork in the road, where Sunday morning, Sunday night, and Wednesday night brought the same crowd of people together each week. David grew up in a similar church that shared the same social circles; therefore, our extended church family was relatively large. Everyone banded together that night in a humbling way. I just made a couple phone calls, explaining the situation, and within minutes, an army of volunteers was making plans to help Ashley and David.

We watched troves of people flood our house. With little instruction, people spread out and began assembling furniture, cleaning, washing baby clothes, and organizing Harley's room. Someone ordered pizza and boxes began to stack up in my kitchen, people grabbed slices as they worked. My Type-A nature screamed to step in and refold a few items or rework arrangements at times, but my heart overflowed with gratitude. Clearly these people had lives. They had families, jobs, and responsibilities and yet they dropped everything at the last minute to come help us. I looked around and saw two of my friends who had just had babies themselves folding tiny layettes and onesies fresh from the dryer. Another friend, Ashleigh, sat on the floor of the nursery putting together the glider. The nursery wasn't a life or death matter. Harley would never have known if his room was finished or not, but all of these people knew that it mattered to David and me.

With all of the hustle and bustle around the nursery upstairs, I didn't even notice my dad quietly working downstairs.

Tommy: *When your child is diagnosed with cancer, there isn't a whole lot you can do to help. You feel helpless. When we walked into Ashley and David's house that night, I knew there was something small I could do. See, in our family, we love Christmas – all things Christmas. At our home the serious business of decorating for Christmas begins in October in order to have everything fully decorated before Thanksgiving, with me leading the charge. The crown jewel of my Christmas decorations is the Christmas village, which was always one of Ashley's favorites.*

I knew with everything going on, Ashley wouldn't have time to put out any Christmas decorations. She just had too many other things on her mind. As everyone else worked in the nursery upstairs, I slipped into the garage and gathered all the boxes and bins labeled "Christmas" and got to work. I wanted to surprise Ashley. She would be expecting the nursery to be finished, but not the

Christmas tree and decorations. I hoped having her house decorated would not only bring some holiday cheer into their home, but also be a small spot of normalcy in the midst of all the other chaos going on.

My jaw dropped as I walked down the stairs. Christmas had erupted in my living room. The Christmas tree lit up the space, shining in spite of the bins and tops littered around it. Stockings were hung and candles burned in each window. Tears streamed down my cheeks as I walked toward my dad. I wrapped my arms around him and sunk my head onto his shoulder. As people hustled around us, I savored the moment as I felt like a kid again, aching for the protection of my dad against the pain in my life. His thoughtfulness in the midst of such turmoil touched my heart deeply.

At the end of the night, we had a complete nursery, a beautifully decorated house, and felt more support and love than most people ever know or experience in a lifetime. We could not adequately express our thankfulness that night as people left, but no one seemed to care or even notice. They strolled out as casually as they had strolled in, not expecting anything in return.

Despite being physically exhausted, sleep eluded us in the eerie darkness of our bedroom with only faint moonlight seeping through the curtains. I rested my head against David's chest. His heart beat methodically while mine beat wildly. My eyes, swollen from crying, still managed to produce tear after tear. "Why me?" echoed in my head incessantly. Like Job, I couldn't understand why this was happening to us.

For most people, it is not until they face the most unbearable circumstances that they begin to see their faith for what it truly is. It takes those times when circumstances throw us against the rocks and every bit of the life we've known shatters for us to look around for the hope we say we have. Some people have no clear faith in anything. During the storms of life, they simply fight despair and endless worry, while others have such optimism that they can find hope despite tough circumstances.

David and I were supposed to be in the optimist camp. We had grown up in church our entire lives. We had both made professions of faith in Jesus when we were very young, only to truly place our hope and faith in Jesus later in our teens. We believed the Bible. We knew all the stories. We didn't just attend church on Sunday mornings – we were faithful to every service and involved in numerous activities.

However, I began to realize that my faith was embarrassingly shallow. I had never walked through any type of real trial – I could work out my situations on my own. I left God at church. Prayer was important in theory, but in reality, it was something we did at meals. I talked about prayer more than I actually prayed. People would share prayer requests, and I looked at it more as a time of sharing information, than a time to petition an almighty

God on our behalf. I'm not sure if I knew of a time in my life that God had answered a specific prayer, not because He wasn't able or even that I doubted that he could, but because I never even thought to ask.

David: *Like Ashley, I felt like a "good Christian" before the cancer. We went to church and lived "right." To look at us, we appeared to have it together; however, inside there was an emptiness. I had never really thought I needed God, other than for salvation. Our lives were easy. We had jobs, family, friends, and a little money in the bank. We didn't need to pray for groceries or health or comfort. Those things were in abundance all around us. We devoted minimal time to prayer and Bible study. I knew it was important, but it almost seemed like something that was more important for the pastor to do than for me. We were busy. We had school and jobs and obligations. It's amazing how priorities can shift so quickly when faced with hard circumstances though. My average Christianity suddenly wasn't enough. My wife's, and possibly my son's, lives were in peril. I suddenly needed the anchor that only Christ can give. I didn't know exactly what to do or how to cling to Him, but I knew enough to know to pray and started praying like I never had before. For the first time in my life I understood that I needed God. I needed answers. I needed Him to protect my family in a way that I simply could not. It was out of my control.*

Chapter 8
Cutting the Cord

"For this child I prayed..." I Sam. 1:28

Friday, November 16, 2007

There is something unnatural about knowing the day you will give birth. I pictured a mad dash to the hospital, like you see in movies, with a police escort and barely making it to the room before the baby is born. I flipped through the morning talk shows as I procrastinated, not wanting to pack my bag for the hospital. The aroma of coffee lingered in the air as thin bands of sunlight streamed in between the wooden slats of the blinds. Harley's feet stabbed under my ribs repeatedly, my morning coffee clearly giving him a boost of energy.

This would be the last few hours our house would be so still. Other than Lulu's occasional racket, our home remained pretty quiet. Cries, coos, and giggles would soon fill the quiet pockets of air. Diapers, wipes, blankets, and burp cloths would be scattered about, while Lulu would be searching for the source of interesting new smells.

I blinked back tears, the joy, heartache, and anger mingling down my cheeks. I enjoyed being pregnant – every single minute of it. I loved every kick, hiccup, swollen foot, and rib pain. I couldn't believe it would be over in just a few hours. While I was desperate to meet Harley, I battled the anger building over the situation surrounding his birth. The poor little guy had no idea he only had a few more hours before he would be thrust into the world to a mommy with cancer.

Just a few months earlier, I had been dreaming of going to law school, then I found out I was pregnant. Immediately, the dream of a high-powered career melted away. I couldn't imagine spending my days anywhere other than with my baby. I knew plenty of moms with full-time jobs who made it work, but I just lost all desire to be anything but a mom. I wanted to be the one there to see the milestones and the mundane. I couldn't wait. And I couldn't visualize just one baby in our family photos.

Reluctantly, I stood up to go address the half-empty suitcase on the ground. As I dumped my dishes in the sink, I glanced over to the package on the kitchen table. I grabbed it and walked upstairs. I couldn't risk forgetting it because it could hold the key to my cancer treatment. Just after my diagnosis, Dr. Soundararajan suggested we consider banking the blood from Harley's umbilical cord. Umbilical cords contain stem cells that can be used in research and treatment of many diseases, including some types of cancer. While the chances were slim that it would be beneficial for me, the opportunity seemed worth the cost, except at the time, we simply couldn't afford the $2,000 it would require.

As I researched the cord banking process, I noticed that the company's policy stated the fees to bank the cord blood would be waived when a mother was diagnosed with a list of specific diseases. My heart jumped. Maybe this could be our answer. However, I called the company that afternoon and learned that I would not qualify for the waived fees because my type of cancer had not been determined. Given the circumstances though, they compassionately offered us a reduced fee. Even with the reduced price of $1,400, it still exceeded our budget. A woman from our church heard about the situation and offered to pay for the procedure for us. We were stunned and thankful. I immediately called the company back and ordered the kit. (This incredible act of generosity would be the first of innumerable people stepping in to financially support us through this ordeal.) The company overnighted the package to ensure we had it before the delivery on Saturday.

As I sat on the edge of the bed, I stared at the suitcase on the floor, with only the cord blood package and slippers sitting inside. With the induction set to start at 7:00PM, and a round of pre-op blood work that needed to be completed beforehand, I didn't have much more time to waste. Packing under the circumstances offered none of the excitement I had imagined in connection with packing for the birth of our baby, but I forced myself to gather the necessary items for Harley and me.

With the suitcase finally packed an hour later, I trudged downstairs to finish the dishes I had left in the sink. My eyes fell on Harley's diaper bag, his name monogramed across the front in block, blue letters. My feet froze as my eyes lingered. Its perched position by the front door seemed so natural, and yet our circumstances were anything but normal. I had cancer, and Harley was coming too early. Our "normal" felt like it was being wadded up like a spitball and flung across the room.

Just after lunch, our Pastor, Eddie Wyatt, knocked on the door. Flanking his shoulders stood some of the staff and deacons from our church.

Brother Eddie: *As a Pastor, I often see people in their most desperate hours. There is something within each one of us that calls out to God in our most desperate times. Walking into someone's living room to pray with them is a sobering thing. People are looking to you for answers and comfort and yet, sometimes it's impossible to see. I am thankful I can go in armed with the knowledge of a God that is good and is sovereign and has promised to work all things out for good to those that love Him.*

Seeing young people, like David and Ashley, receive such serious news was heartbreaking, especially since she was pregnant. Knowing that the outcome of our situation lay outside our control, prayer was our only option. James 5:14-15 says, "Is any sick among you? Let him call for the elders of the church; and let them pray over him, anointing him with oil in the name of the Lord. And the prayer of the faith shall save the sick..." That's exactly what we had come to do.

The men and I stood shoulder to shoulder, surrounding David and Ashley. I took out a bottle of simple olive oil and brushed a few drops across her forehead. The oil did not hold any power – it was just plain olive oil from the grocery store – the power rested completely with the Lord. My voice broke with emotion as I began to pray.

My dad's arms squeezed around my shoulders as he took a turn to pray, the graceful, tender words heaving through his sobs.

Tommy: *As a deacon of our church, I had prayed over sick people on many occasions. Nothing, however prepares you to pray over your daughter and unborn grandson. I had watched my own sister die of brain cancer. I knew how cancer can ravage a body and a family. I did the only thing I could do for my daughter in that moment – I called out to the Lord asking Him to help in ways that were beyond my control.*

Like the men standing around me, I had no idea what would happen or how God would answer our prayers, but even in that dark moment, I had an unwavering faith in the goodness of God. Those of us with gray hairs and wrinkles lining our faces had weathered storms that Ashley and David had not had to weather. We had witnessed the faithfulness of God through difficult circumstances. We had seen God miraculously answer prayers at times when it seemed like heaven fell silent in response to our most desperate prayers, but as a father, I had never had to watch one of my children endure such pain. I prayed that the Lord would be close to her and carry her through the storm too strong for her earthly dad's arms to bear.

Tears stained faces as they said good-bye and turned to leave. The door closed softly and our house fell silent once again. The Christmas tree glowed in the corner as our living room grew dark, the fall sun setting earlier each day. I placed three remaining silver ornaments on the Christmas tree, hung Harley's stocking next to ours on the mantle, and managed a few smiles for some final pregnancy pictures.

We arrived at the hospital at 7:00 PM and got settled in our room. I smiled as the steady rhythm of Harley's heart beating flooded the room as the monitors were put in place along my bulging belly. My parents and brother stopped by to drop off a basket of snacks overflowing with hordes of chips, pretzels, crackers, cinnamon streusel muffins, hard candy, mini candy bars, gum, and bottled water. At the time, the size of the basket seemed overkill for just David and me, however, as visitors poured in over the next few days, the basket was quickly depleted.

The medical staff administered Cervidil that night to help prepare my body for labor the next day. They also gave me a sleeping pill to help ensure I would get some rest that night, knowing I would have a long few days ahead of me. David and I took a few quick pictures before I drifted off to sleep.

Saturday, November 17, 2007

I woke up at 2:00AM with sharp pains wrapping around my back and across my abdomen. I struggled to take more than a few shallow breaths as the pain continued. I was groggy enough from the sleeping pill that I wasn't clear what was going on at first. I called the nurse and she confirmed that I was having strong contractions. I believe God had been preparing my body all along to give birth early. The pre-term labor and contractions had apparently been great preparation for being induced at 33 weeks. I labored on my own for a few more hours, received my epidural, and then around 8:00AM they started me on Pitocin to help regulate my contractions. Everyone was prepared for a long day. Inductions are not always quick, especially so early in a pregnancy.

Around 11:15AM, my doctor said I was about 5cm and she was happy with my progress. She assured us it would be several more hours, probably late afternoon, before we would have a baby. With that news, everyone took the opportunity to go grab some lunch while there was still time.

Sheila: *I immediately volunteered to keep Ashley company so everyone else could get something to eat. I can never eat in situations like that anyway – lunch was the furthest thing from my mind. I didn't want to be anywhere other than by her side, just in case she needed something. I paced around the room, attempting to walk off my nervous*

80

energy before finally forcing myself to pull a chair over next to Ashley's bed.

I curled my legs underneath my blanket, turning on the TV, as I assumed I had hours to kill before anything exciting happened. As my hand pressed against the bed for support to reposition myself, something changed. Only five minutes had elapsed; my nurse hadn't even had a chance to leave the room. The epidural masked any pain, but I felt an intense pressure, an urge to push.

"Um, I think I need to push," I sputtered.

"Well, you were just checked. It's probably just a strong contraction."

Straightening my arm against the bed, I raised up, half expecting to see a baby lying on the bed beneath me. I thrust the words across the room: "No, I need to push, *now*!"

My mom jolted out of the chair, but the nurse calmly told me that she would see if my doctor was still in the hallway. Clearly, she wasn't feeling the same urgency that I was feeling. As she sauntered toward to the doorway and down the hall, I thought, "Take your time sweetheart. It's no problem. My momma's here. She can catch this baby."

A few moments later my doctor reappeared, snapping her gloves on as she walked over toward my bed. My mom resumed pacing. I'm sure my doctor thought I was overreacting, but as soon as she checked me, her countenance changed.

Our entrance to the hospital the night before may not have been a mad dash, but the next few minutes made up for it. Her eyes widened and she jumped off the stool, barking orders to anyone that would listen. In the frenzy of the moment, she seemed more like a 250lb drill sergeant, than an 85lb doctor.

"She's a 10! He's coming!"

It suddenly went from just my mom and me to countless nurses and staff hustling through my room. The mood was more chaotic than the average delivery's because Harley was so early. We also wanted to store the cord blood, and nothing was prepared for that either. I became frantic with worry that David would miss the birth. I was certainly in no position to delay though – Harley was coming, and he was coming now.

David: *My parents and I decided to go grab a quick bite to eat in the cafeteria. I knew I needed to at least try to eat even though my emotions were all over the map. We hadn't even made it to the cafeteria before Ashley's mom, Sheila, called and told me to hurry back. I was confused but rushed back upstairs. The room had transformed into a beehive of activity. We were about to have a baby. Everything else swirling around us faded away for that moment.*

Seconds after David walked in, the doctor told me I could push. Unlike many first-time moms, for me, the pushing was the easy part. I have big hips, which I have learned comes in handy when having babies...not so much when you are buying swimsuits, but amazing when you are birthing babies. Just three pushes, and he was born.

The medical team had prepared us for the worst, for the fact that he may not be breathing or that he would be blue. So, I was shocked when they laid a screaming, pink, tiny baby on my chest. Nothing could have prepared me for the joy of that moment. He was perfect. His tiny little hand rested right on my heart. It was as if he was telling me everything was going to be okay. I just wanted to freeze time in that perfect moment.

David: *Watching Ashley give birth to our son was overwhelming. She was battling cancer, totally unsure if she would live or die, and yet she made birthing a baby look effortless. Harley seemed fine, but with everything they had prepared us for, it was impossible to know for sure. After Ashley held him for that sweet moment, they whisked him over to the warmer. I nervously watched the nurses' faces, searching for any clues to his condition as the doctor, a neonatologist, examined him.*
No one was rushing around or seemed concerned – that gave me hope.

Just a few minutes later the neonatologist gave us incredible news: "Your baby looks great. He is breathing fine on his own and is maintaining a good body temperature. I see no reason to take him upstairs to the NICU."

We were shocked. He said he had never seen a baby born so early not have to go to the NICU for at least observation. Tears ran down my cheeks as they handed our 4lb 11oz little boy to me. The nurses encouraged us to use skin-to-skin contact as much as possible to help keep his body temperature up. Time with my son was precious, given what I would be facing in the coming days. Knowing he could stay with us was the best news we could hope for. As he lay on my chest, his hat brushed against my chin, I could feel his little heart beating against mine. That harmony seemed to drown out the buzz around the room.

My eyes came to rest on Dr. Soundararajan across the room as she inserted the needle into the umbilical cord meticulously. I watched, mesmerized by the incredible skill required to extract blood from such a tiny piece of human flesh. She carefully stored the blood and packaged it in the kit. David had arranged for a courier to arrive right after the delivery. There was not a moment to lose when dealing with cord blood. We had no way to know if the investment would pay off, but in that moment we were thankful to have it waiting should we need it.

After the team of doctors left the room, my nurse told me I could try feeding Harley. I sat up and positioned myself and him. For something that should be so natural, our first attempts did not go as well as I had envisioned. My anxiety increased as I knew my time to hold him and nurse him would be far less than I desired. The nurses encouraged me to keep trying and assured me that it would get easier.

After the attempted nursing session, we were escorted from the delivery room to a mother/baby room in the postpartum wing. As soon as we rounded the corner toward our room, I could hear voices. I felt like Moses parting the Red Sea when the nurse wheeled my bed through the room. The people stepped back, creating just enough room for my bed and Harley's bassinet to squeeze in. I feel confident there was a visitor policy that we grossly exceeded. Knowing the status of my health and upcoming surgery, the nurses must have overlooked the rule pertaining to the number of visitors allowed during our stay.

Sheila: *Through the midst of all the excitement, I struggled to share in the joy around me. I couldn't have been more thrilled with Harley and how well he was doing, but I couldn't take my eyes off Ashley. My baby was still sick and that loomed larger than anything else in my world.*

The excitement in the room was palpable, but then I had to leave. An orderly standing by the door could barely be seen around the throng of people.

"Time for your MRI."

My heart sank. Now that I had delivered Harley, I was a full-time cancer patient. Immediately after the final push when Harley was born, the knot had exploded in pain, maybe due to the rush of adrenaline or hormones coursing through my body. It throbbed relentlessly, feeling like the size of watermelon.

85

It was hard to believe that my doctors had still never seen a clear picture of it. The slides from my biopsy and the physical exam were the only tools they had up until this point to hypothesize what the tumor looked like. Since the MRI wasn't possible while I was pregnant, they had been anxiously awaiting the moment that one could be performed. As I left the room, my heart was broken and my body was tired. An MRI was the last thing that I wanted to do. It was like being put in time out at your own birthday party. I fought back tears as I was turned to leave. The noise level was so high that I'm not sure if everyone even knew that I had left. The crowd of people surrounded Harley's bassinet as they wheeled me out, shutting me out of one last glimpse.

I lost track of time as the MRI drug on and on. My stomach churned with hunger pains. My heart ached to see Harley and hold him close. The doctors wanted an image of every possible angle of the tumor. Obviously no one could be with me during the procedure, but I desperately wanted news about how Harley was doing. Was he hungry? Was he sleeping? Did he need a diaper change yet? To my relief, after what felt like hours, everything was complete and I could go back to my room. I envisioned a peaceful nap with Harley snuggled up by my side.

As they opened the door, my vision of a peaceful evening had to be altered, but that was okay. Tons of family and friends still encumbered the space. I was grateful to have so many people who wanted to show their love and support for us. I was ready to embrace the celebrative atmosphere until I saw what was taking place. I blinked my eyes to make sure it wasn't a dream.

In the corner of the room a nurse stood over Harley. David, my parents, and my in-laws were gathered around his bassinet. Everyone else pressed closer to see. The video camera was in David's hand. He was laughing. The room chirped with excitement. The nurse wrapped him in a towel.

Harley had just had his first bath.

I was livid.

My heart beat wildly and my face reddened. They had to ask people to move to even get me into the room. Furious thoughts raced through my mind. "How are you giving my child his first bath, while I'm downstairs getting an MRI because I have cancer?!?" I could not fathom why no one had thought that I would want to be present for such a special occasion. Maybe to someone else it would have been just a bath – something we would repeat hundreds of times in his childhood – but to me it was much more. Given my diagnosis I knew I would miss so many moments of Harley's life; there would be unavoidable times that I would be fighting for my life. This was different. This was avoidable. I didn't have to miss this. I could have been there. They could have waited. Why didn't someone just say, "No, let's wait for his mom to come back."

I felt like I had been forgotten and the pain seared my heart. My emotions were so raw with fear and nervousness that not getting to participate in my child's first bath tipped my emotional scale. It was like I was drowning in a room full of people. I felt guilty for being so angry when everyone around me was so joyful, but I felt robbed.

When David's eyes met mine he knew something was wrong.

David: *As a first-time dad, I was completely clueless about the schedule of events in the hospital or even how to take care of a baby. The nurse came in and said that Harley needed a bath. I said, "Okay," and didn't think twice about it. Looking back, I should have told her to wait until his momma got back. I got caught up in the moment and should have stopped to consider Ashley's feelings. I grabbed the video camera, knowing she would want to record the moment, but failed to consider the pain she would feel over not being there.*

The crowd started to disperse shortly after the bath and eventually David and I were left alone with Harley for the first time. Harley continued to have trouble nursing. My eyes burned with tears as I fought to get him to eat. Feelings of failure pierced my heart as I watched my helpless son struggle to suck. The nurses told us that his sucking mechanisms had not fully developed. To help him eat, they gave us tiny straws to use while supplementing formula. Holding the straw in his little mouth was an awkward, tedious process. Despite our best efforts, it was difficult to get him to eat. We silently wondered if maybe he should have gone to the NICU, maybe they could have cared for him better than we could.

By the middle of the night I was a mess. The emotions of the day, hormones, and lack of sleep caught up with me. In a fit of tears, I cried out to David, "I just want my mom."

Sheila: *As new grandparents, we were just wading into the waters of learning when to offer help and when to give Ashley and David privacy. After we left the hospital for the evening, I kept my phone right beside me, sitting on go, ready to go back to the hospital if she called. Around 9:30 my phone buzzed and I had it to my ear before the first ring ended. I teared up when David asked me to come. I had my purse in my hand and headed for the door before we ended the call.*

Once I helped get everyone calmed down and fed, I sat in the chair holding Harley and urged Ashley and David to get some rest. As I rocked my tiny grandson, so perfect from head to toe, I prayed.

"Dear God, I need you right now. My baby girl is sick and You are the only hope we have. This little boy needs his mama. I feel so helpless. I'm her mom – I should be able to fix this, but I just can't. When she was little and would come to me with a boo-boo, I could kiss it and make it better. This is beyond my ability. Only You can help her. Please, dear Jesus, heal her body."

89

Visitors continued to flood our hospital room the next day. We enjoyed the time as much as we could between blood work, nursing shift changes, hospital food and endless poking and prodding. Being discharged Monday morning brought welcomed liberation. The November air was crisp as they rolled us out to our car. Harley weighed in at a whopping 4lb 8oz that morning. The car seat far outweighed him. David pulled around and loaded us up for the half-hour drive home. When we pulled in the driveway, a fresh round of tears filled my eyes. No matter how short our time would be at home, I knew we would savor every moment.

The next morning, we took Harley in for his first doctor visit. Over all, for a 33-week old preemie, he was doing remarkably well. Our pediatrician, Dr. Beckford, communicated two concerns: his weight and his temperature. We needed to be diligent to keep those two things from dropping. His weight, already down to 4lb 4oz, needed to start trending upward.

Between packing for another hospital stay, feeding Harley, crying and praying, we did not get any significant sleep that night. Harley was just three days old and I was a bundle of nerves. While I was concerned about the surgery, I did not want to leave my son. I had just started to get to know him. I knew he would be in excellent hands, but my heart was grieved at the precious hours and events I would miss. I had been a mom for four days. It wasn't enough time.

As I laid down that night, fear gripped my heart. I set my alarm for 4:00AM. David drifted off to sleep and I stared at the ceiling, tears streaming down my face. I prayed to a God I had known about my whole life. I wished my prayers were visible so I could see if they even made it past the ceiling. They felt that feeble. But in that moment, I had to trust in a God I couldn't see to do something impossible that I could not control.

Chapter 9
Cutting Out the Cancer

"The Lord is my strength and my shield; my heart trusted in him, and I am helped; therefore, my heart greatly rejoiceth; and with my song will I praise him." Ps. 28:7

Wednesday, November 21, 2007

A few months into our marriage, someone advised us to take out a life insurance policy. He explained that we could lock in low premiums by taking out the policy while we were still young and healthy. We pursued taking out a small policy for each of us. A few weeks later, a lady came to the house to complete the basic medical tests the company required before issuing the policy. They certainly don't just take your word that you are healthy.

She wore purple scrubs and lugged a caddy and scale up the steps to the front door. She sat across from us at the kitchen table with a clipboard stacked with questionnaires. She fired off question after question, shoving her pen through her short brown hair, tucked neatly behind her ears, as she filled each new page. Next, she took our blood pressure, weight and then prepared to draw our blood. David went first since I didn't enjoy the sight of blood and needles. When my turn came, I adjusted my chair and held out my arm. The needle pierced my vein with precision and then it was over. The whole process only took a few minutes and then she left.

I never dreamed how routine vitals and blood work would one day become. I also never dreamed I would be so thankful for a life insurance policy. I guess thoughts about things like life insurance policies and funeral arrangements are somewhat inevitable right before surgery to remove a cancerous tumor, but they seemed out of place while holding a precious new life. I rested in the glider that our friends had put together the week before. Harley's tiny body lay nestled against my chest, his head tucked under my chin. His rhythmic breathing mimicked my own as we sat in the quiet darkness. We had only been home for two days. Nursing still felt challenging, but I knew my nursing days were short, so I fought discouragement over not getting it right. Two days at home wasn't long enough. I yearned for time with him, for more time to be a family and get adjusted to life together.

I heard footsteps downstairs. I knew it was time to go, but I couldn't seem to pry myself out of the chair – as if the weight of sorrow pressed against my shoulders. It seemed impossible to stand up. It had been over a week since my last full night of sleep and my body felt completely drained. The knot under my jaw ached. Dark circles crept further and further down my cheeks.

Eventually David stepped into the room. "It's time."

My shoulders heaved and tears trickled down my cheeks. He braced my arm and helped me out of the chair, and I walked down the stairs. As my eyes met my mom's, the silent tears turned into loud sobs.

Patsy: *Even though Ashley didn't share my blood, she felt just as much like my child as my boys did. She was our family and it was heart-wrenching to see her in such emotional pain. No woman should have to have surgery days after giving birth when hormones are sky-high already. Sheila and I nestled Ashley between us as our tears flowed freely. As helpless as we felt for Ashley, we knew we could do our part by making sure that Harley was cared for. I was scheduled to sit with Harley until Krista came to relieve me in time for me to make it to the hospital for the surgery. We all just pitched in, filling in the gaps the best we could.*

David stood silently as the women cried around him. He knew we needed to leave for the hospital soon, so he focused on that mission. I held out my arms and Patsy gently took Harley. Dr. Parks indicated that I should only be in the hospital for two nights. Unfortunately, that would mean missing Harley's first Thanksgiving. I knew he would be well taken care of, but it broke my heart to leave him.

David had been by my side tirelessly during the past week protecting me, providing support, and letting me cry. He was the rock that I so desperately needed. However, his responsibilities suddenly doubled.

David: *I felt torn. I wanted to be with my wife and support her in any way that I could. As I looked into the tiny face of my helpless son, I knew I needed to be with him too. Just the day before, at his first doctor's appointment, our pediatrician, Dr. Beckford, showed some concern over his weight, down to 4lb 4oz, and his borderline body temperature. In that moment, however, I had to trust Harley's care to my mom and Krista in order to focus my attention on Ashley.*

We climbed into the car for the hour-long trip to the hospital. My shoulders shook with convulsions as I cried while red, puffy bags surrounded my eyes, a physical evidence of my anguish. I pressed a Kleenex to my raw nose for the thousandth time that week. David's hand rested against my shoulder.

"Ashley, you have to gather yourself. People at the hospital are going to think someone has been murdered. Harley will be fine. Everything will be fine."

At his urging, I attempted to compose myself as we walked in the doors of the hospital. My mom, my dad, and David's dad, Richard, were already seated in the waiting area with other friends and family. I thought of our cruise together, which seemed like yesterday and a lifetime ago, when my biggest concern was my swollen feet. My palms oozed with sweat. David and I were shown to a small pre-op room. I changed into my hospital gown and took the only seat in the room – a small chair in the front corner. I shifted anxiously as the minutes passed and the room began filling up with my family and a few close friends. Brother Eddie, our pastor, stood once again to pray over us. Everyone was crying, yet his voice managed to press through the emotions. His calm, steady words provided stability and confessed the dependence on the Lord we all felt. After the prayer, everyone solemnly filed out of the room and headed back to the waiting area, leaving David and me alone.

A parade of doctors and nurses rotated through the room, each repeating questions like – when was the last time you've eaten? The nerve doctor who would assist in the surgery stopped by. He explained that to help ensure the facial nerves surrounding the tumor were preserved as much as possible, I would be hooked up to a machine that would map the nerves in my face and guide the doctors in real time through their maze during the procedure. At last, Dr. Parks appeared in the doorway. His blue scrubs were a clear sign that the time was near. He walked through the surgery one last time with us, explaining that it should last 2-3 hours.

"Do you have any questions?"

I blinked back a new wave of tears as I said, "No," while endless questions flashed through my brain.

"We'll take good care of you," he said turning to leave, his scrubs brushing the curtain as he walked away.

A few minutes after he left, two nurses came to take me to the operating room (OR) – time to say goodbye. I hugged my family. My mom's release was reluctant. I kissed David, and mouthed the words, "I love you," for I had no power left in my voice. His smile through tears gave me the strength I needed to pull my glance away.

I walked next to the nurse down the hallway, unconsciously counting the tiles on the floor as they went by. The mid-morning sun filled the hallway with light as we turned the final corner toward the OR. A florescent glow filled the room, a stark contrast from the sunlight beyond the doors. Machines and monitors beeped and buzzed in every corner. A dark-haired nurse, not much older than me, helped me onto the operating table. Although the air felt chilly, my limbs trembled as adrenaline coursed through my veins.

One by one the medical team greeted me and introduced themselves, their names often muffled beneath their surgical masks. Between their greetings, I prayed. I had nothing new to offer to the Lord; tears and prayers had been my constant companions over the past several days. As I stared up at the drab ceiling tiles, my final plea to God was to protect my son and David if I didn't wake up.

When Dr. Parks and the rest of the necessary medical team were assembled, the anesthesiologist covered my nose and mouth with a mask. My eyes locked on his as my chest rose and fell with deep breaths. "Count backward for me and picture in your mind an amazing vacation you want to take when you get out of here." My eyes rolled unintentionally as I thought, "Sir, you may want to rethink your speech for cancer patients. A nap in a chemo chair is the closest thing to a vacation I will probably get for a while." As I slipped from consciousness, my thoughts shifted, "I should be back in my room by lunchtime."

David: *Dr. Parks had told me to anticipate the surgery lasting 2-3 hours. As the third hour came, my stress level, which was already high, increased exponentially. I continued to check with the receptionist, but each time was told that there was no update on Ashley's surgery. I probably wore a hole in the carpet pacing the small path available through the crowd, which had grown to over 80 people. After sitting in the waiting room for over six hours, we were all on edge; I knew something must be wrong. Finally, my questions were answered with the news we had been longing to hear – Ashley was out of surgery.*

As Dr. Parks stepped into the waiting room, the crowd of friends and family rushed to gather around him. I pushed through and he asked if I wanted to go somewhere more private to discuss Ashley's condition. I knew he would relay the information to the crowd of people better than I would later, so I told him it was fine to talk with everyone else around.

"The tumor was the size of a softball. It had finger like extensions that wrapped around her jawbone and into the jaw muscle. We scraped the bone, took portions of her

jaw muscle, and lymph nodes. We took everything on the right side of her jaw that we could take."

A stunned silence hung in the air. Everyone's eyes were fixed on Dr. Parks as he further explained that in order to remove the tumor, a facial nerve had to be cut. He would not know the extent of the potential damage until Ashley was out of recovery.

Through my broken states of coherence in the recovery room, I thought, "I'm alive." Relief washed over me. As my bed rolled out of the recovery ward, my relief turned to dread. In the once sunlit hallway, I could see the moonlight filtering through the trees. Something felt wrong – why was it so late? Just as I started to ask the nurse for the time, I heard a loud, almost primitive scream.

Sheila: After Dr. Parks had left, we all sat around, anxiously waiting for Ashley to be moved out of recovery. I moved outside the waiting room and leaned against the glass windows in the hallway. The tension inside me had built up like a pressure cooker, ready to explode. I just wanted to see Ashley and know she was okay.

I scanned the hallway in the direction they had wheeled her that morning, the cream walls soon blending with the floor and the ceiling as my gaze tired. Suddenly, I saw her. I bolted down the hallway, desperate to reach her before she reached the next set of doors. I grabbed her hand and cried, "Ashley, it's Mom. I'm here, Ashley. Love you baby." Her bandaged neck turned slightly toward me, but I couldn't tell if she could hear me. Her hand fell to the bed as it moved outside of my grasp. The door closed behind her, leaving me standing alone in the hallway.

I shuffled back down the hallway. David met me outside the waiting room, initially scolding me for not letting him be the one to see Ashley first, but his frustration quickly faded. Much like the bath incident with Harley days before, I hadn't even thought about what I was doing – I just reacted when I saw her. Ashley was okay, and that's all that mattered, we agreed. Later David even chuckled, commenting "I know If that had been Harley being wheeled out of surgery, Ashley would have bulldozed through a crowd to get to him first too."

With emotions heightened, the entourage followed my bed into the room. My bed's incline was set high enough to keep me comfortable due to the drain that had been placed in my neck during the surgery. David, our parents, and my brother lined the wall as the nurses secured my IV and checked my vitals.

Dr. Parks looked somber as he entered the room a few minutes later.

"Will you smile for me?"

I thought, "What? Why on earth does he want me to smile?" I complied. As my lips turned upward, even on both sides, his face relaxed, his shoulders fell with a sigh of relief and he reciprocated a smile. "In order to get all of the tumor, we had to cut a facial nerve – the nerve that controls your ability to smile. Cutting the nerve was simply a risk we had to take to ensure that we removed all the tumor." Instinctively I smiled again, eager to double check my ability myself.

He went on, "The tumor was mistaken for a salivary gland because it had positioned itself directly over the gland and had grown into it, but we are confident we got it all." The confidence he expressed over getting good margins around the tumor was a welcomed relief.

By the time Dr. Parks left, it was after 8:00PM, the night before Thanksgiving. I insisted to David that he leave and go home to be with Harley. He wanted to stay with me, but I desperately wanted Harley to have at least one of his parents home with him on Thanksgiving morning. Finally, David agreed and my mom settled in for a night at the hospital. My body and mind were equally exhausted, but the drain in my neck made it difficult to get comfortable in the hospital bed.

Although I could not save my milk due to the medication I had taken, I still needed to pump every three or four hours in order to maintain my milk supply. I didn't know if I would ever be able to nurse Harley again, but I wanted to at least give myself the opportunity. Throughout the night, my mom would selflessly get up and pump for me. The weight of exhaustion on my body allowed me to sleep through most of the pumping sessions. Even though I had only been a mom for a few days, watching my mom take care of me that night gave me an even deeper appreciation for what it meant to be a

101

mom. I wanted to be there for Harley in the same way my mom was there for me.

The next morning, sadness filled my heart as I woke up. Not only had I spent my first night away from my son, but it was Thanksgiving morning. What should have been a joyous celebration with family and friends, had to be a somber time with our family fractured. The nurses, housekeeping staff, and lab techs who shuffled in and out of the room all wished us a Happy Thanksgiving, but I could barely muster a response. I simply wanted to crawl under the covers, go back to sleep, and wake up at home beside my husband and son.

Later that morning, my dad joined us. My mom flipped the TV channels between morning news shows, each one with table decorating or last minute recipe ideas, and the Macy's Thanksgiving Day parade. My sadness only deepened when my lunch tray arrived. I lifted the lid on the tray to reveal two pieces of sliced turkey with grayish-brown, lukewarm gravy. Over-cooked carrots, stuffing, and stewed apples rounded out the plate.

David and I were somewhat at odds that day as well. He naturally wanted to be with me and help care for me after surgery, but Harley could not come to the hospital. Since he was premature, we could not risk exposing him to any additional germs. Harley had to stay at home, and I wanted him to spend Thanksgiving with at least one of his parents. My sadness over not being with Harley felt so intense, that asking David to stay home with him was the only course of action I could entertain.

David: *Although my family still got together for Thanksgiving dinner, I did not want to take Harley out of the house, and I honestly didn't feel like being around a bunch of people. My mom brought over a plate of food for me and visited with me for a little while. I flipped through college football games as Harley rested on the couch in the living room, but I struggled to focus on anything other than Harley and thinking about Ashley at the hospital.*

Dr. Parks surprised me when he stopped by after lunch. I hadn't anticipated him making rounds on a day when he could have been spending time with his family. His kindness was evident in his decision to come check on me. He examined the drain in my neck and informed me that if everything went well, I could go home the next day. Since I was more coherent than the night before, he reiterated his assessment of the surgery.

"We got clear margins on your tumor yesterday. I am confident we got it all. Once we determine what type of cancer it is, we will know more, but there is a possibility you will not need radiation or chemotherapy treatments." We thanked Dr. Parks for taking time to come see me. My mom gave him a hug for both of us.

His assurance felt like a ray of light shining through my dark cloud of sadness. I had real confidence that this situation would work out despite my current circumstances. The pain of being away from Harley on his first Thanksgiving was countered with the hope of being with him for all the ones in the future.

Later on, I relented and agreed for David to leave Harley to come see me. As a mom, I wanted him to be with Harley, but as a wife, I understood that he wanted to be with me, as I would have wanted to be with him if the tables were turned. My parents took the opportunity to take a walk and get some decent food. I soaked in every detail David could tell about spending Thanksgiving with Harley.

Around 5:00PM my dinner tray arrived. I'm sure the hospital staff intended to make patients' Thanksgiving dinner memorable, and they certainly succeeded! David and I chuckled when we saw what they had brought me to eat. With drain tubes coming out of my neck and a chart which stated I should be on a soft-foods diet, I was served a piece of cube steak that looked more like shoe leather than food. I tried to cut it, but the entire piece of meat slid with my knife across the plate. I did not want to seem ungrateful, especially on Thanksgiving, but gnawing on a piece of beef jerky after having a portion of the right side of my neck removed wasn't how I wanted to spend my evening.

The next morning, I was bursting with anticipation to go home and be with David and Harley. The only thing standing between me and freedom was the drain in my neck. A nurse came in after rounds and gave me a dose of pain medicine. As she handed me the pill she whispered, "You're going to need this."

When the medicine had time to kick in, she came back in to remove the quarter-sized drain from my neck.

"Take a deep breath. This will be pretty uncomfortable."

She pulled. I closed my eyes and gripped the bed rail so tightly, my knuckles turned white. The excruciating pain ended as the long tube snaked its way out. I gasped and coughed to catch my breath as the nurse gathered supplies to bandage the hole left in my neck. My mom's eyes briefly filled with tears as she watched the painful process. However, I willingly endured the pain that would bring me one step closer to being at home with my son.

As I signed my final discharge papers, David and Patsy were taking Harley in for a follow-up appointment to ensure he had not lost any more weight since his appointment on Tuesday. While my dad navigated the winding, tree-lined streets approaching our neighborhood, my stomach fluttered in anticipation. Despite having had a baby and surgery, I almost sprinted up the stairs to the door. Lulu greeted me, her tail wagging ferociously. My feet paused briefly as I flipped my shoes off, breathed in deeply, and silently thanked the Lord for bringing me home.

By the time I showered and put on fresh clothes, my mom had already started a load of laundry. I settled onto the couch and anxiously awaited the phone call from David saying they were on their way home. My phone rang a few minutes later.

"Hey Ashley..." David's tone sounded ominous. "Um, Ashley, the doctor needs to talk to you."

"Okay, let me talk to her." My eyes locked with my mom's in the silence as David handed the phone to the doctor.

"Hi Ashley, it's Dr. Beckford. I have little Harley here with David and Grandma. I am so sorry for the week you have had. Unfortunately, Harley is not doing so well. He is continuing to lose weight and his body temperature is really low. We are not able to keep it up to where it needs to be. He needs some care that only the hospital can give. I have recommended to your husband that we admit Harley to the PICU (Pediatric Intensive Care Unit) where they can help regulate his body temperature and monitor his feedings."

I lost it. The anticipation of the last two days shattered into heartbreak. My shoulders heaved as I fought to maintain enough composure to listen to the doctor.

"Oh honey, I know you were so looking forward to being at home with him, but this really is the best thing for him. I wanted to be the one to tell you. You are his mother, and we don't want you to feel left out of this process since you couldn't be here today. Bringing him straight to the hospital really is my recommendation."

"Okay," I heard myself stammer. What else could I say? What could I do? Of course, I wanted my son to get the care he needed, but the blow took me to a dark place.

As clouds of anguish descended I felt like our string of bad news would never end.

"I've asked David to take him directly to the hospital to be admitted..."

"...without you," the storm in my brain whispered.

I questioned God's plan. It was bad enough that I had cancer, but for my son to be struggling felt like too much to bear. My prayers screamed from the depths of my heart to God, asking him to take away the pain and suffering we were enduring.

David: *I knew Harley was not doing well when we took him to the pediatrician's office that day. He just wasn't eating well, despite our best efforts. I had only been a dad for a few days, but I knew enough to know that something wasn't right. His tiny little body struggled to take in food. His weight was just 4lb 4oz – down seven ounces since birth. When Dr. Beckford told me that he needed to go to the hospital, I crumpled. I pictured Ashley sitting at home, waiting patiently to hold our son, and I knew the devastation that this would bring her.*

Dr. Beckford's sensitivity to the situation was incredible. She volunteered to talk to Ashley personally as she could see I was in no shape to do it myself. Then after her phone call with Ashley, she turned to me. My shoulders hung down as I sat in the chair holding Harley, tears dripping off my chin. In a movingly powerful moment of humility, she knelt down, oblivious to the dirt and germs that must have covered the floor, and prayed. Her strong, encouraging words brought comfort to my heart. She was not only an excellent doctor, but as a believer, she anchored her hope and faith for our family in Jesus Christ alone.

Patsy: *Dr. Beckford's prayer was a bright light in a dark, depressing situation. As I stood next to my son, so desperate to do something to relieve his heartache, I was humbled by this doctor's prayer. It showed me God's grace even in that moment. Harley was a beacon of hope and source of joy for everyone touched by Ashley's cancer, like God's daily reminder that He is the giver and sustainer of life.*

David: *My mom and I left Dr. Beckford's office and drove straight to the hospital where we got settled into a room and the nurses advised me to keep him under the heat lamp or on my chest at all times to maintain his body temperature. I cringed as I watched them prick his heel to draw blood. His little voice cried out in such pain. Then they snaked a feeding tube up his nose and down into his stomach, his little body wrestling to get free. I wanted so desperately to take his pain and Ashley's pain and bear it myself. I felt helpless.*

Later that evening, as I sat in the chair, holding him skin to skin, Ashley walked into the room. I stared at my wife – her neck bandaged from surgery and her body exhausted from the events of the past week – and I was in complete awe of her strength and determination. Every doctor told her not to come to the hospital, but she had relentlessly pleaded with her parents to bring her so that she could hold Harley.

She walked in and sat down on the bed, her red jacket stood out against the white sheets. I placed Harley in her arms, and the care of the weeks seemed to evaporate for just a moment. It was not how we pictured it – holding Harley together as a family in our living room – but for that brief moment, we were all together and things seemed right. The interlude had to be short though as we knew Ashley could not stay at the hospital overnight. Her tearful good-bye pushed me to pray and ask God why all of this was happening to us.

I was once again torn between wanting to be with Ashley and wanting to be with Harley. They both needed my care and attention, but circumstances forced me to stay at the hospital with Harley and see Ashley only for brief times when someone would bring her to visit. After five grueling days, Harley had improved enough to be discharged. Feedings were still tedious, but we were elated to go home. As I drove us home I prayed that this would be the last hospital stay for our family for a long time.

Chapter 10
Clawing for Control

"What time I am afraid, I will trust in thee."
Ps. 56:3

December 2007

I sat in the glider, looking over at Harley sleeping in his crib. At three weeks old, he had just begun filling out the preemie-sized clothes. The love that I felt for him overwhelmed me and exceeded what I ever anticipated was possible. How could I love a little person so much? Yet, even in that moment, just weeks after giving birth and having surgery, a hole in my heart ached for more children. Maybe I would have felt the same desire even if I had been healthy, but given the treatment options looming on the horizon, my fear of losing control slowly took over.

My battle against cancer seemed to be at a standstill. After the pathologist at Kennestone analyzed the slides, the type of cancer could not be determined. The slides were then referred out to the Mayo Clinic in Minnesota, a leading center in pathology. Dana Farber Hospital in Boston, a specialty center for sarcomas, eventually examined them as well. No one could reach a definitive answer about what kind of cancer I had.

With each passing day, I worried that the option of more children would be taken away from me forever. As my world spun through a vortex of chaos, I crawled and grappled for anything I could control. David and I wrestled with the decision to attempt to harvest my eggs. I had tunnel vision to preserve the possibility of future children. It consumed me. The postpartum hormones raged in my body and probably helped to magnify the problem in my mind as I pushed and pushed, paying no heed to the warnings and counsel of those around me.

David: *I went along with the decision to find a fertility doctor because Ashley was so adamant about it, but at the time, I couldn't have cared less about having more children. I was okay with the idea of Harley being our only child. My only concern was to have a healthy wife and a healthy son. What was the point of worrying about having more kids in the future if Ashley didn't live through this cancer? I wanted to do what was best for Ashley and didn't see how putting her body through fertility treatments and IVF (In Vitro Fertilization) could be good for her.*

Sheila: *Tommy and I stood in firm opposition to Ashley's idea to harvest her eggs. I couldn't imagine why she would want to put her body through such an ordeal right after surgery and as she faced cancer treatments. It seemed selfish. She had a husband and son who needed her now. I didn't want to see her pump herself full of hormones that could possibly fuel her cancer even more. I just didn't understand her resolve given the risks. All I could do was pray as I quickly saw that her mind would not be swayed with reason. I prayed that any remaining cancer cells would be numb to the hormone fuel she was willingly pouring on the fire.*

At the time, I couldn't see the cause for the deep concern. In my mind, I was cancer free. My doctors told me the tumor was gone and the margins were clear. I refused to let any preventive treatments ruin my chances for the family that I had always dreamed of. The pushing, the insistence, and the bulldozing through road blocks felt more like determination than recklessness. The fear grew in my heart from a seed of anxiety to a thick, gnarled tree of desperation.

I let the voices of doubt and self-preservation take the steering wheel of my life. I allowed the dark season of my life to be further clouded with these dark whispers of doubt, like Eve listening to the snake describe the tantalizing yet deadly fruit dangling over her head. I didn't bother to dig deeply enough into my heart at the time to see the root of the problem – trust. I didn't trust that anyone or anything could fix the situation other than me.

I was blind to the fact that while I prayed, went to church, and read my Bible, I did not trust God. I could not place my future in His hands and release the grip I thought I so firmly had. The subconscious decision to overlook God's sovereignty in my life and for my family led me down a path to disrespect and disregard the wisdom and emotions of those I cared most deeply about.

So, I pushed. Choosing to ignore Dr. Miller's instructions, I pursued finding a fertility specialist that would help us harvest eggs before any chemotherapy treatments began. It shames me painfully now to admit that I never prayed about the decision to harvest my eggs. While I rammed the circumstances together to achieve my goal, the Lord's ever present hand of mercy followed me through the prayers of my family. I knew our window of time before treatments began would be extremely limited, which made finding a doctor who would agree to work with my condition even more pressing.

The first week of December, David and I checked into Dr. Fogle's office. The cascading waterfall and plush carpets created a serene atmosphere. It reminded me of my oncologist's waiting room, almost as if comfort and beauty of the room was a small attempt to ease the pain of cancer or infertility. The office's policy of not allowing children made for another afternoon away from Harley, but I felt he was meant to have siblings, and this was the only way I could see to make sure he got them.

We each took a seat in front of a large, dark-stained desk. I noticed the family pictures scattered around the room of Dr. Fogle and those I assumed to be her husband and three sons. Sadness and a touch of bitterness surged through my heart. I wondered if she had struggled to conceive – if she knew the struggle that each one of her patients faced. Even the nurse that led us down the hallway looked as if she would be delivering a baby any day. Did she understand the loss that I anticipated – the loss of the ability to bear children? I battled these thoughts as I shifted in the chair: I had just given birth. I had never known the pain of infertility in the classic sense, but the loss I felt seemed very real. The loss of a dream.

Dr. Fogle greeted us with tender kindness and southern charm. With her long hair cascading across her shoulders, she listened to my story. As she prepared to explain our options, she paused. I could sense the hesitation in her voice as she articulated her concerns, given our circumstances. I marveled as I pondered that God, the Creator and giver of life, had equipped doctors like her to help couples birth new lives into the world. The tone in her voice conveyed that she did not take that responsibility lightly. She expressed concern over giving me hormones that could fuel my cancer and apprehension over helping us create embryos that I may never live to see mature. However, seeing the determination I exhibited, she agreed to help us with one cycle. Given the pressing time constraints for treatments, we had one shot.

She went on to explain that in order to harvest enough eggs for fertilization, I would need to begin hormone injections to stimulate my egg production. The eggs would then be harvested and fertilized. The resulting embryos would then be stored for later use. This was precisely the solution I hoped for. It felt like a tiny sliver of life that I could control. With stored embryos, I knew our chances for having future children, no matter what my course of treatment, would be secured.

Before we left, we were given papers regarding what we wanted to be done with any unused embryos should the situation arise. Three options appeared on the papers before us: discard the embryos, donate them to scientific research, or donate them to a couple for adoption. We believed strongly that the Bible teaches that life begins at conception – those embryos would be human lives. Discarding the embryos would be like throwing away our own children or donating them to become human science experiments. Neither of those options were possibilities for us. The remaining option, however, made us uncomfortable as well. Donating embryos to be adopted would mean that we could have biological children walking around one day whom we did not know. Thankfully we were able to take the paperwork home to consider our options.

While we went home to be with Harley, I asked David's dad to go to a pharmacy across town to pick up the medication and injections. From the kitchen, I heard David answer the phone, "No, Dad, that's right. I know...I know it's a lot of money." The $4,000 price tag was shocking, but it felt to me like a small price to pay for the security of future children. I suppressed the uneasy feeling of the financial hardship that transaction would cause. The desire for control felt so overwhelming that I was willing to pay whatever it took to follow my plan.

The stimulation process was grueling both physically and emotionally. I took the oral medications each day and gave myself the hormone injections every night. At first, David had to help me inject the hormones into my stomach; they were incredibly painful. I was literally pumping my body full of what the doctors were saying was possibly the fuel for my cancer, but I welcomed the thought of something other than cancer growing in my body. As I cradled Harley, I would dream of the future children we would one day have. I did not allow myself to think of a future for him without me in it.

The following week, we returned to Dr. Fogle's office for an ultrasound to determine how many eggs could be retrieved and harvested. My stomach fluttered with excitement and anticipation. I felt so confident walking into the office that day, knowing that cancer wouldn't take this away from me.

My brown boots clicked down the hallway as we turned the corner into the ultrasound room. Expecting to see Dr. Fogle, I was surprised when an unfamiliar, tall, male doctor walked in. I lay on the table, prepared for an internal ultrasound and my joyous anticipation turned to distress at the idea of a male doctor I had never met preforming such a personal procedure just four weeks after I had given birth. My cheeks flushed, and I grabbed David's hand as I strained to calm my nerves.

A few minutes into the procedure, the doctor's face turned from warm and friendly to cold and indifferent. I wondered what could be wrong.

"I have some bad news. The hormone injections are intended to stimulate egg production to allow us to harvest enough eggs for the IVF cycle. Unfortunately, in your case, instead of producing multiple eggs, the hormones produced only one egg – what we call a 'super egg.' This happens sometimes and unfortunately there is nothing we can do. This is a failed cycle."

The doctor hustled out of the room. Tears began to flow down my cheeks, sobs bellowed out of my chest, and I wept like never before. David wanted to help me up, but I could not stand. The only relief I felt was at least now we didn't have to decide what we would do with any unused embryos.

My solution had fit neatly into my box of control. I had followed the directions precisely, spent more money than we had to spend, and possibly fueled lingering cancer cells in my body – for what? A failed cycle? Once again I faced the harsh reality that I had lost control. Finally, it occurred to me to pray – if you can count screaming from the soul as praying. I screamed at God, questioning why this was happening. At just 26 years old, I had cancer, a premature baby, and would be barren the rest of my life. This was not the Sunday School picture of God that I had formulated in my mind.   It felt like He had either failed me or just didn't care.

Chapter 11
Bitter Cold in Boston

"Evening and morning, and at noon, will I pray, and cry aloud; and he shall hear my voice." Ps. 55:17

A week after the heartbreak of the failed cycle, we were just wrapping up Harley's newborn photography session when the phone vibrated in my back pocket. It was Dr. Miller. My eyes met David's as I stood up to answer the call. After three hours of coaxing a newborn through a photo session, we were already exhausted.

We had been expecting her call. Five weeks had passed since my surgery, and we still had not been told what kind of cancer I had. My parents had come to see Harley's photo session, but with the anticipation of Dr. Miller's phone call, they had been a bundle of nervous energy all afternoon, especially my mom. My mom started crying before Dr. Miller even had an opportunity to start talking.

I slipped out of the lobby and into the cool December air under the walkway, to avoid making a spectacle in the waiting room of the studio. My white shirt billowed with the breeze as I held my breath, bracing myself to receive the news. I felt the eyes of the other clients in the waiting room boring into my back as the door creaked open and my parents followed me outside. With the hormones from the failed fertility cycle still raging in my body, the emotions of the situation seemed to be amplified, like trying to give a presentation after pulling an all-nighter. I had nothing left.

I turned my back and saw my friend AngeLeah's parents drive across the parking lot and ease up to the curb next to where my parents were standing. My mom rushed to the car window as it lowered exclaiming, "We're about to get the news. We're about to get the news." As I fought to keep my focus on Dr. Miller's words, I noticed my mom starting to cry again as she leaned next to the car window.

I grew more flustered with every passing moment – so much for not making a spectacle! I longed for the privacy of my own living room to process this news and discuss the information with David. Yet, I stood on a sidewalk, in the midst of a photo session, with eyes on every side and my family and friends crying just steps away.

I pressed the phone closer to hear above the noise of passing cars. "The people at the Mayo Clinic believe that it is angiosarcoma, which is a rare type of soft tissue cancer that resembles blood or lymphatic vessels. The Dana Farber Institute in Boston would be the best place for you to be seen since it is the center for expertise in sarcomas."

Given my age and the tumor's location, Dr. Miller originally thought I had some type of lymphoma, a much less aggressive form of cancer. The word "rare" echoed through my mind as I struggled to process this dramatic shift in diagnosis. Twenty-six-year-old women don't get sarcomas. They are too rare – it seemed impossible. Once again, I wondered, why me?

Dr. Miller continued, "I know it's a lot to process, but with such a rare type of cancer, your best course of treatment is with the experts in the field. I will let you know when we can get you an appointment in Boston."

"What did she say?" my mom asked frantically as I hung up the phone.

"They say it may be angiosarcoma. They aren't sure though. If it is, they want us to go to Boston to a see sarcoma specialist," I snapped coldly.

At this news, my mom lost it. In retrospect, I would understand. Standing on a sidewalk, she found out that her daughter might have a rare, aggressive form of cancer. However, in that moment, I wanted to maintain my composure, finish the pictures, and leave. I walked back in the studio, wiping tears from my face and pressing my words out in an effort to keep my voice from shaking.

"David, I need my parents gone. We need to finish this session and I just...I just need them to leave."

Sheila: *I paced back and forth on the sidewalk, trying to contain my nerves while Ashley talked to the doctor. The anticipation for this news had been mounting for weeks. Ashley stood just feet away, getting news that would change our future. I could sense Ashley's irritation building as the emotions escalated. I fought to keep it together. I didn't want her to feel like she had to take care of me when*

I should be the one helping to take care of her. Nothing can prepare you for your child being diagnosed with cancer. There is no manual on how to act or what to do.

When David asked us to leave, we understood. We all needed some time to process the news and we respected their desire for privacy. Every step of the way, all we wanted to do was provide them with the support they needed. If they wanted us to leave, we would leave. If they had wanted us to stay, we would have stayed.

I sat numbly inside while I bounced Harley, my feet swaying as I rubbed his tiny back. Once again, I felt control slipping through my fingers and chaos begin to swirl around me. I frantically brushed away tears as I watched my parents turn and walk toward their car. I just wanted to go home.

The following week, Dr. Miller secured an appointment for me at the Dana Farber Institute in Boston. While we were thankful for the opportunity, the logistics of getting to Boston seemed overwhelming. Since Harley was so little and his health and immune system still fragile, he wasn't able to fly. Both sets of parents wanted to be there to support us, but someone needed to stay at home to care for Harley. We decided that our moms would stay with Harley, while our dads would go with us to Boston.

Our budget had already been stretched after I had to quit my job for bed rest in October, and with the cost of the fertility treatments, we did not know how we would pay for four last-minute tickets to Boston, especially the week before Christmas.

When Dr. Parks, the ENT that had performed my surgery, heard about our situation, his office offered to raise the money to pay for our plane tickets. We were overwhelmed by Lord's provision and their generosity. Our needs were being met almost before we had the opportunity to ask. Since I didn't want to be away from Harley any longer than necessary, we decided to fly up to Boston and back on the same day on the following Tuesday hoping the answers we wanted would be found there.

Tuesday, December 18, 2007

As we had left the house that morning, I kissed Harley's forehead, thankful his eyes were still closed, and I adjusted the monitor's volume level to make sure my mom could hear it when he woke up. The moon still shone as we pulled into the Atlanta airport after a quiet ride – no one felt much like talking so early in the morning. I gathered my bags and thought of nothing but Harley as we walked through the parking lot toward the shuttle that would take us to the front door.

I let my eyelids fall as the plane taxied, hoping to catch a quick nap during the flight. In addition to cancer, surgery, and the failed round of fertility treatments, I was still a mom of a newborn, which made sleep a precious commodity. As I drifted in and out of sleep, I prayed that we would be given good news. The wait to begin treatments had been agonizing. We feared the unknown

122

– what type of cancer I had, whether it was really gone, whether it would come back, what treatment options we would be given.

When the plane began to make its decent into the Boston area, I noticed sweat droplets lined Richard's forehead. I often lost sight of the how difficult the situation was for our family. All the sorrow, worry, frustration, and fear that David and I felt was not in a vacuum. Our families felt it as well.

Richard: *The day in Boston was the worst day of my life. The intense nerves, anxiety, and worry I felt on the inside could be seen on my face. Our family faced such devastating news with Ashley's diagnosis. These kids, now parents themselves, were looking to us for comfort and support. I just felt an unbearable sadness every time I looked at Ashley and thought about David and Harley. I knew the Lord was in control, but I just didn't see how this situation could end well.*

As we broke through the clouds, a breath-taking view of the city blanketed in snow came into view. Growing up in the south, I had never experienced more than an inch or two of snow. I almost felt as if we were on a vacation eagerly anticipating the sights and sounds of a new city in the snow--a reprieve from the sadness and turmoil at home. Then, reality slapped me in the face when I got off the plane and the bitter cold air pierced through the fresh scar on my neck. I remembered the circumstances that had brought us there.

The shuttle snaked away from the airport, through the narrow, snow-covered roads toward the Dana Farber Institute. I reached for a snack in my bag. Even though it was well before lunchtime, my stomach growled, my pre-dawn breakfast long gone. When we arrived at our stop, we pushed through the bitterly cold wind until we spotted a Starbucks on the corner and filed in, eager to fill our hands and stomachs with something warm. We poured over a map, trying to get our bearings and determine which way we needed to walk.

Outside, I pulled my jacket over my cheeks in a vain attempt to block out the bitter wind. Apparently the day was cold even by Boston standards. As southerners, we felt like our extremities were going to freeze. We found the Dana Farber building and dashed through the revolving glass doors. I double checked my paperwork for which floor we needed and as the elevator climbed, so did my heart rate.

Huge glass windows surrounded us as we stepped off the elevator. Since we had a few minutes before my appointment, we walked around the beautiful facility and stopped in a small shop that sold scarves and wigs. I couldn't picture myself ever needing one, but the clerks handed me a few scarves to take with me once they found out I was a cancer patient. The red scarf reminded me of a wall in our house I had once convinced David to paint in honor of his favorite team, the Georgia Bulldogs. After the eight coats of paint it took to achieve just the right shade, I had to vow I would never ask him to paint anything in our house red again.

We eventually weaved our way toward the reception desk. Gentle snow fell outside as I sat in the vast waiting area with row after row of chairs filling out a mountainous stack of paperwork – the arduous task made me feel as if I were applying for citizenship to another country. In the crowds of people that ambled past the desk, I could pick out the cancer patients; they were the frail, thin looking ones without any hair. Looking at them felt like looking in a crystal ball at my future. At last, I walked the clipboard back up to the receptionist and took a seat again as close to the window as I could get. I distracted myself by looking out the window and watching the snowflakes drift to the ground far below. I dreamed of being carefree – making snow angels on the puffy white mounds of snow – free from the weight of cancer.

Close to an hour went by before my name was called. The lab work and procedures before I could see the doctor were arduous. The nurse led us across the hallway to a small exam room. I felt as if I stretched my arms out, I could have touched both walls. Cramming four people into the room made it feel even smaller.

The sarcoma specialist opened the door and adjusted his glasses as he walked behind his desk, sat down, and rolled his large chair toward the desk.

"Good Morning," he said, his Boston accent as thick as our southern drawls.

125

"Sarcomas are nasty. They are aggressive and some are extremely rare. Unfortunately, more than likely, yours is both."

My palms started sweating, and the walls felt like they were closing in. We talked for quite some time about my surgery and the possible sarcoma that lived inside my body. He wanted his team of pathologists to look at my slides and see if they could give a definitive diagnosis. He expressed concern that the surgeon didn't remove enough of the tissue and lymph nodes in my neck during the resection.

This was not the answer I had expected. He continued, "I would also like for you to meet with one of our head and neck surgeons to determine if more surgery will be necessary. Even if we get the cancer in remission, there is a high chance it will come back. I want you to begin radiation and chemotherapy. Ideally, it would be best for you to move here to Boston for at least six weeks to complete your radiation therapy and begin chemotherapy."

After all of this, his final blow was a bit of well-intended, but devastating advice. "In case you don't own one, I would buy a good video camera. Make lots of videos for your son."

David: *Just five weeks before, we had hoped that this cancer journey would be short – the tumor was gone, and Ashley might not even have to have chemotherapy. Now this oncologist completely uprooted all those hopes and exchanged them for dread. I went to Boston expecting this specialist to have an exact treatment plan, and he simply gave us a lot of hypotheticals and worst case scenarios. When he told us to get a video camera, I wanted to get up and leave his office. Maybe he was right, but after traveling all the way up the entire east coast to see him, I just expected something more.*

We later found out from Dr. Miller that he did have a more specific treatment plan, but not one he was willing to share with us at the time. He believed so strongly that the surgeon hadn't removed enough tissue around the original tumor, that he wanted to perform a radically, disfiguring surgery by removing part of Ashley's jaw bone. Dr. Miller vetoed this idea; therefore, it was never presented to us.

We had flown all the way to Boston to see this doctor, and now I could not do the one thing he asked me to do – move to Boston for treatment. Harley would be too little to fly for a while and being from the South, we would never want to navigate driving that far in the winter months. I knew the only hope I had for any treatment to be successful was if I were with Harley. Being apart from him would eat away at me worse than any cancer could.

I mustered my courage and objected. "I need to find a radiation oncologist in Atlanta," I told him.

He peered through his glasses at me as if to say, "Are you serious?" He just didn't understand that I could not do this without my son by my side.

The brutal wind blasted us as we exited the building. Lunch time had come and gone while we were at the appointment, so we searched for something to eat and settled on a diner down the block. It was a hole-in-the-wall place, but had surprisingly great food. I had pizza while David felt the cultural pull to have a bowl of clam chowder, which turned out to be a perfect choice on the cold, wintery day.

As quickly as it had begun, our trip to Boston came to an end. We had gone with high hopes of receiving a treatment plan and came home empty handed. Once again, we were asked to wait. So much for regaining the control I so desperately craved.

I think I opened the car door before David even turned the engine off. I rushed in the house and cradled Harley in my arms while filling my mom, Krista, and Patsy in on the events of the day. When everyone had gone home for the night, I rocked Harley to sleep and thanked God for precious moments I could spend with him. For a few hours that night, I managed to forget about treatment plans, biopsies, and tumors. Through the moonlight, I drank in the sweet smells and sounds of my baby boy and prayed for many, many more moments together.

Chapter 12
A Mother's Vision

"And he said unto me, My grace is sufficient for thee;
for my strength is made perfect in weakness..."
II Cor. 12:9

"Sleigh bells ring, are you listening? In the lane, snow is glistening..." The sounds of Christmas accosted my ears as I dashed into Target, eager to escape the cold drizzle that had just begun to fall outside. It was December 23. Ordinarily, I would have had all my Christmas shopping completed well in advance of the holiday, but shopping had been the furthest thing from my mind. Fighting for my life put fighting crowds into a new perspective.

I weaved in and out of the aisles grabbing last minute gifts and snacks to take to family Christmas celebrations and pushed my cart toward the check-out line. With each passing face and each friendly smile, anger began to well up inside me. I wanted to yank down one of the speakers chiming Christmas tunes and scream, "Does anyone know what I'm going through? I have cancer! I had to give birth to my son eight weeks early, and he's still not strong enough to eat like he should. Oh, and by the way, I can't have any more children! My dreams are shattered, I may be dying, and you people are buying gifts and Christmas candy like nothing's going on!"

The words of the clerk jolted me back to reality, "Excuse me, ma'am?" I thrust the cart forward and dumped my items onto the belt as I checked out, wrapped the bags around my wrists, and walked outside, thankful for at least a break in the cold drizzle.

Over the next few days we endured Christmas celebrations. Living so close to both sides of our family fills our schedule with endless get togethers – grandparents, great-grandparents, aunts, and uncles were all eager to share in Harley's first Christmas. However, a sadness hung in the air, dampening the festive spirit that typically permeated our home and extended family. It certainly wasn't what I pictured for my son's first Christmas. We tried to make the best of the situation and enjoy the time with Harley though. Despite the circumstances, this would be the only first Christmas he would ever have.

Lunch at my grandmother's was followed by one of my favorite Christmas traditions (and probably David's least favorite). We gather around my parents' tree on Christmas Eve to open one gift, which happens to be the same gift every year: pajamas. Flannel, fuzzy, jersey, or sleek – for 26 years I had gone to bed on Christmas Eve wearing my new Christmas pajamas. My pink, jersey-knit pjs stood in appropriate, feminine contrast to David's masculine, moose-printed flannel pants. Harley joined the tradition when we unwrapped red snowman pajamas. We scurried up the stairs to change. Despite being a newborn size, the fleece fabric bulged around Harley's torso as we curled up on my parents' sectional couch, the lights of the

Christmas tree flickering against his rosy cheeks. For a brief moment, the trials that had plagued our life in the past few weeks faded among the tinsel, lights, nativity scenes, and ribbon-wrapped gifts.

The next day, at David's parent's house after Christmas lunch, my sister-in-law, Krista, handed me a small red package. I slid my finger under edge of the carefully folded paper, tearing it off the box to find an iPod. I couldn't have imagined a more perfect gift! Anticipating long hours of treatments, hospital stays, and doctor visits, songs flipped through my mind as I planned out the playlists I would soon create. My petulance over the Christmas music at Target seemed silly after such loving time with family and such a thoughtful gift.

Thoughts of my own health situation got shoved completely aside the day after Christmas. I could hear Harley breathing from across the room, his clogged nose making a crackling, gasping noise with each breath he took. His first cold seemed too big for his tiny body already, and it had just begun. I chided myself as I knew he must have picked it up while we were shuffling between parties over the past two days. The next day, his cold began to develop into something even more. I knew something felt wrong as he struggled to eat due to his respiratory symptoms. The thick mucus in his nose forced him to breathe through his mouth, which made feedings even more tedious than they already were. By mid-morning he had eaten less than an ounce. As he lay nestled against my leg on the couch, my eyes followed his

131

blue striped pajamas, watching to make sure he kept breathing. Lulu sat at my feet, almost as if she could sense my growing concern.

I called the pediatrician's office, but they couldn't see him. The nurse told me if I felt his condition needed more attention than we could give him at home, we should take him to the ER. With David at the fire station, my parents offered to go with me. The doctor sent us home, stating that Harley had a virus that just needed to run its course. I'm sure the doctor attributed my concerns to being a first-time mom

However, by early evening, worry consumed me as I watched him breathe, and he hadn't eaten anything all afternoon. I threw the diaper bag in the car and returned to the hospital, determined to get him help. Once again, we were turned away. My mom tried to soothe my growing anxiety and offered to stay to keep watch with me over Harley that night. Neither of us got much sleep.

After enduring hours of watching my son suffer, my fingers hammered the numbers to the pediatrician's office at exactly 8:00AM. It was really just a formality though. I would show up at their office even if they told me no appointments were available. My son couldn't breathe. He needed help.

After a brief examination, my motherly concerns were validated. The doctor admitted Harley directly to the hospital from the office due to RSV – Respiratory Syncytial Virus. She explained that while it can be mild in some children, other cases, like Harley's, needed care that could only be given at the hospital.

Relief washed over me. I was thankful that the pediatrician took the necessary steps to get him help; however, it seemed surreal that we were preparing for yet another hospital stay – our family's fourth in six weeks. I insisted on staying with Harley, since I couldn't during his previous hospital stay, due to my cancer surgery. Since David was at work that day, my parents brought clothes and necessities for me while Harley and I settled into his room. Two deep blue chairs sat positioned against the window with a white metal crib against the wall. The large window overlooked the parking lot, a less than exciting view.

Over the next few days Harley's condition gradually deteriorated rather than improving. His tiny chest struggled with every raspy breath. The nurses would come in to help with his bottle feedings and administer breathing treatments as IV antibiotics hung over his bed. He had always struggled to eat well, but feedings became almost impossible. The nurses would coax down his formula, drops at a time, by tilting his head in order to relive some of the congestion and allow him to swallow more easily. One dedicated nurse displayed the patience of Job. She was so kind to us and loved on Harley as if he were her own. Shockingly, he would even eat for her. I don't know how or why, but he would drink the whole bottle if she fed him.

Nurses, doctors, techs, janitors, food service staff – someone was always coming and going from Harley's room, which made sleeping more than a couple hours at a time extremely difficult. Time crawled. In the quiet moments, I read a book Krista had given me called *Crazy Sexy Cancer* by Kris Carr. Krista had already highlighted and marked places for me to read and take notes. With my cancer diagnosis still in limbo, I welcomed any avenue to educate myself about my health and my disease. Information felt like power.

The sunlight warmed my back as I sat by the window reading one morning. Harley had just fallen asleep when my right eye started hurting. The dull ache radiated from deep in my eye socket. My fingers swept across my eyelid. It felt bruised. I wondered if I had hit my eye during the night somehow. An emerging headache made me even more uncomfortable. I chalked it all up to lack of sleep and attempted to continue reading. A few minutes later, a knock at the door signaled the time for Harley's next feeding. I put the book on the table and rubbed my eye in an effort to relieve the pain, but it persisted. That night my mom could see the discomfort wearing on me, and she offered to stay awake with Harley to give me the chance to sleep. Every time I woke up, the pain was just as severe as it had been before I went to sleep.

After the nursing shift change the next morning, my eye pain intensified. It felt as if liquid was being pumped into my eyeball, causing intense pressure.

Turning my head brought on a sharp, cutting sensation deep within my eye. It felt strange – like nothing I had felt before. Walking out of the bathroom, I steadied myself with my hand on the wall as the room seemed to shift, and everything doubled.

"Mom, there are two of you."

"Well, aren't you lucky," she chuckled.

Sheila: *At first, I just chalked up Ashley's double vision and eye pain to stress compounded with the lack of sleep from having a newborn in the hospital. It was not surprising that her body was reacting that way. As the afternoon progressed though, her eye pain got worse, despite me forcing her to rest in the chair. I knew a friend at an eye clinic near the hospital, and she got Ashley an appointment. I felt sure though, that above anything else, she just needed some rest.*

When David arrived at the hospital, I had to explain why I needed to go across the street for an appointment at 2:30. His reaction mirrored the nurse's and my mom's. He felt sure that the stress and fatigue of battling cancer was taking a toll on my body. He assured me everything would be fine, and I appreciated his optimism.

A puff of air hit my eye, as the doctor, sitting just on the other side of the machine, checked the pressure in my eye. It was the final test over the course of 20 minutes.

"Everything looks normal. Given the amount of stress you have endured in recent weeks and the lack of quality sleep, I'm sure the pain in your eye is just your body's way of telling you to slow down. My guess is that when things settle down and your body has a chance to relax, your eye pain will go away," he said with a confident smile.

Back at the hospital, the news that my eye pain was stress-related eased my mind but did not help alleviate the discomfort or headaches associated with it. I took a couple of ibuprofen and focused my attention on Harley who, despite the doctor's best efforts, continued to get worse. His little body, curled up under a navy-blue blanket, fought for every breath.

On Monday, New Year's Eve, the doctor informed David and me that Harley would be transferred to the Children's Hospital in Atlanta within 24 hours as his condition needed more specialized care. As I made phone calls to inform our families about the upcoming move, I packed my bags.

2007 had been a roller coaster of emotions, from the immense joy of becoming parents to the searing pain of a cancer diagnosis, including the possibility of never having more children. As the sun began to set, the nurses told me not to anticipate the transfer that night. With the holiday, it would more than likely happen the following day, and I was glad. I wanted to usher in the new year with my little family, just David, Harley and me. As we watched the ball drop, hope pierced the sadness that surrounded us.   David held my hand as we lay crammed on the two uncomfortable blue chairs, and he prayed for our family, asking the Lord for health and healing for 2008. My hand stretched through the bars on the crib to stroke Harley's tiny back as I whispered my own prayer and I struggled to shove aside the question: "Why us?"

The next morning, David left for work straight from the hospital, anticipating a busy 24-hour, holiday shift while my family prepared for their annual New Year's Day feast.   My mom's New Year's Day menu rivals Thanksgiving, including pork tenderloin, collard greens, black eyed beans, rutabagas, corn bread, and of course a selection of her famous home-made cakes. Since my mom couldn't bear the thought of us missing out on the feast, she packed up trays of food for us. Krista came to keep me company, and David even got to stop by for a few minutes during his shift because he was driving a support vehicle that day.

After we had gorged ourselves on the southern feast, it was time for the transfer. Lifting Harley out of the crib, the nurse carefully navigated the cords and tubes, to place him in the enormous incubator for transfer. It made him look more like a baby doll than a seven-week-old infant.

The wheels clanged as they loaded the machine onto the ambulance, and I climbed in the front seat. The driver talked incessantly during the 30-minute drive, her thick southern accent filling the cab, but I barely heard a word she said. The bumpy drive through the rare Atlanta snow fall amplified the pounding in my head. I turned to look at Harley. I could see his crumpled face crying out, but I heard nothing. The sealed incubator silenced his cries. It was heartbreaking. As I continued to turn to look at him, my eyes struggled to focus. As we rounded the curve toward the children's hospital, the buildings outside the window seemed to multiply. A few seconds later, the images morphed back together.

Inside the hospital, Harley continued to wail. It had been hours since he had eaten, and I reached into my bag for a bottle.

"I'm sorry honey, but you can't feed him until the doctor sees him. It's hospital policy."

Irritated, I explained that it had been hours since he had eaten and he was hungry. I wouldn't let my baby scream in hunger. He needed to eat. She seemed to sense my determination and finally said, "I'm just going to turn my head and let you take care of your baby." Harley struggled through the mucus clogging his nose to swallow drops of formula. He only managed an ounce before collapsing against my chest in exhaustion. I felt like crying, but I was too tired for tears, and at least I had done something.

David: The next morning, I went straight to the hospital after my shift. Ashley had been living at Harley's bedside for a week while I was bouncing back and forth between work, home and my family. I hugged her as we stood over Harley. Scenes from a terrible accident I had worked the night before flashed across the TV screen over our heads. A family had been killed, including their infant son. I have worked hundreds of accidents, and while each one weighs on me as a first responder, that one reminded me of how incredibly blessed I was. Even with my son in the hospital and my wife battling cancer, I was thankful to just be with them that morning.

Over the next three days, Harley's condition remained stagnant. His ribs, almost visible under his miniature hospital gown, pushed the tubes as he strained to breathe. The bulb syringe seemed to do little against the avalanche of mucus that filled his nose. The more we suctioned, the less it seemed to help. I scrutinized the numbers on the monitors, concerned that his oxygen level would continue to fall as his little lungs labored to take in air. The doctors prepared us for the possibility that he would need to be placed on a ventilator in order to give his body a chance to rest and heal.

Even though the room seemed spacious at first, after spending a week inside, the walls felt like they were inching closer and closer together. In the tiny bathroom, I stood at the sink, staring at my eye in the mirror, desperate for the constant pain to ease. What had started out feeling like a bruise now felt more like a vice. The hospital bed in the center of the room felt useless at first as Harley obviously wouldn't need it; however, I appreciated the ability to lie flat while the pain in my head and eye mounted. David and I even squeezed together into the railed, twin-size bed to avoid sleeping on the rigid couch under the window.

The next day David came down with a sinus infection and bronchitis, adding to our family's misery, which prevented him from coming to the hospital anymore. My family set up rotating shifts to sit with me and Harley. Thankfully, Krista was able to extend her visit and come to the hospital frequently. Her expertise as a Pediatric ICU nurse was invaluable during that time. Not only could she translate the doctor lingo, but the knowledge she brought into the room gave me incredible peace and comfort.

Friday, January 5, 2008

As the days crawled by, the pain in my head continued to increase. One afternoon, Harley's pulmonologist stopped in the doorway of his room, and there were two of him. I pressed my palms against my eyes, frantically rubbing, desperate for them to refocus. Nothing worked. I couldn't tell which one was the actual doctor and which one was my double vision.

"There are two of you," I explained when he looked at me questioningly.

His concern shifted from my son to me, and he urged my mom to get me to a doctor immediately. My mom was on the phone before he even left the room. I crumpled onto the couch. Hot, fat tears streamed down my face as the doctor left the room. My body folded in half and my head touched my knees as I desperately tried

140

to find a position that would bring some relief. The pressure in my eye was so intense that it felt as if it might force my eye out of its socket. My fingers clutched thick strands of my own hair while my mom's voice drifted across the room.

A friend recommended we try to get an appointment with Dr. Spector, a neuro-ophthalmologist, whose office was providentially across the street from the children's hospital. I could hear the concern in my mother's voice as she pleaded with the receptionist, "You don't understand. She has to be seen today." She stepped out into the hallway, this time calling my dad. "Tommy, please, please call them. Do whatever it takes to get her an appointment. Something is seriously wrong. They say the doctor has to leave at noon, but he has to see her today. Ashley can't endure this pain until Monday."

Tommy: *I called Dr. Spector's office immediately, asking for an appointment for Ashley. I was met with the same resistance my wife had faced. I was told there was absolutely no way that Ashley could be seen, the doctor's schedule was completely booked. I knew I couldn't give up. As I continued to explain the situation, I broke down.*

"Ma'am, you just don't understand," I choked out through my intense sobs. "Something's wrong. Something is really wrong with my daughter. Please, you just have to see my daughter." I kept talking as long as she would listen and she finally replied, "Hang on just a second. Let me see what I can do."

I think I held my breath until she came back on the line.

"Sir, we can work her in at lunchtime. Can she be here then?"

I broke down in a renewed round of sobs, thanking her for listening and taking time to make a difference for our family. I called Sheila and Ashley to let them know what time to be at the office. In the stillness and quiet of my truck after I hung up, I cried out to the Lord.

"Lord, thank you. Thank you. I know You made that appointment possible. I will praise you in the little things, in the good things and in the bad. Lord help us."

To make it to the appointment, I knew we would have to leave Harley alone, but my dad assured us that he would be there soon. I leaned on my mom to stand up, fighting to steady myself, feeling like a drill was boring through my eye.

We made it across the street and collapsed on the long edge of the c-shaped chair formation in the waiting room. A basket of neglected toys sat along the corner of the wall, and I tried helplessly to bring it into clear focus. A couple moments later, I sprinted to the bathroom, barely making it inside before I threw up violently, the unrelenting pain now coursing through my entire body. I trudged back to my chair, and my mom rubbed my back as I clutched my head.

A few moments later my mom whispered, "Ashley look at me." The color drained from her face as she spoke, "Does anything feel different?"

"No," I moaned.

"Ashley, your eye isn't moving."

I rushed back to the bathroom and peered into the mirror, but my double vision made it impossible to look directly at my own eye. When I gave up and walked out, through my altered vision I found my mom with her head buried in her hands, softly crying out to God. I understood her pain as I thought of my own days watching Harley suffer.

"Can you open your eye for me?" Three drops fell through my parted eye lids, burning as I instinctively blinked. The technicians performed dozens of test, which took nearly 45 brutal minutes. Finally, Dr. Spector entered. Although I couldn't focus on his face, I noticed his brown suit contrasted against his white hair, neatly combed over to the right side. His grandfatherly demeanor brought me comfort as he gave me some instructions.

"I want you to get an MRI immediately. I'll bring you back in this afternoon when I have the results." He showed us to a little room while they scheduled the appointment.

"Have you had lunch?" he asked.

"No, actually we haven't eaten all day" my mom answered.

"It's not much, but help yourself to anything you can find."

The door clicked shut as my mom opened the refrigerator, pulling out a Coke for herself and a Sprite for me. She slid a tin of Christmas cookies across the table, the kind with the warm, cozy scene printed around the lid and the cupcake wrappers inside, neatly stacked with an assortment of cookies. I closed my eyes as I sipped the Sprite and ate the cookies. A few moments later he returned, gave us the appointment information and ushered us toward the door. He had a charity golf tournament scheduled for that afternoon, and I knew our appointment compressed his timeline for the day.

After the MRI, we returned to find Harley's room full. My dad, Patsy and Krista were waiting. When the doctor called that afternoon asking us to return for the results, my mom offered to stay with Harley while my dad went with me to the appointment. It was the first time she voluntarily stayed behind. I could see the fear on her face even through my impaired vision and her forced smile.

My dad held my arm as we walked across the street in the cool December air. The fear of more bad news felt magnified because David wasn't with me. I wanted his calm presence as I peered into what I was sure was another tunnel of darkness and despair. During that week, I struggled with the Lord and wondered why so many problems were being poured out onto our family at once. I had cancer. Harley had been in the hospital for a week. David was in bed with a high fever. Once again, the sands of control were slipping through my fingers faster than I could maneuver to hold them.

Dr. Spector canceled his appearance at the golf tournament his own office had organized. His brow furrowed deeply as he pulled up my MRI scan. Right there, glaring against the black edges of the image, glowed a vivid white ball.

"Is it cancer?" I uttered before he had the chance to explain.

"Yes," he sighed, "even without further testing, I'm sure it is."

Dr. Spector stepped out for a few moments to give us some privacy to process the news. I collapsed into my Dad's shoulder, both of us engulfed in a wave of emotion. I felt sure this had to be the bottom of the rocky, dark cavern we had been flung into.

Tommy: *As Dr. Spector delivered the news, I didn't look at him. I looked into my daughter's face. No one should ever have to see their child receive that kind of news. As her daddy, I was the person that was supposed to protect her from the world. I felt utterly helpless and devastated. I wanted to take her pain and put it on myself. All I could do was pray, "Lord, help us. You've got to do something."*

Eventually Dr. Spector returned, patiently waiting for us to regain our composure.

As I pulled myself together, I fired off my next question, anxious to make a plan: "So, do we operate? When can you operate?"

His eyes locked on mine as silence filled the room, his hesitation measurable.

"Oh Ashley," he said quietly. "I'm sorry, but your tumor is in a place only God's hands can go."

I stared at the white ball of tumor and saw my life, my family, and my motherhood. All of it bound in a place where only God's hands could rescue, and I wondered how to trust those hands.

Chapter 13
Losing Sight

> "In my distress I called upon the Lord, and cried unto my God..." Ps. 18:6

When my dad and I had returned to Harley's hospital room from Dr. Spector's office later that afternoon, my mom, Patsy, and Krista stood huddled in a corner near Harley's bed. As I slipped past my dad, Krista lurched across the room, flinging her arms around my neck. We all cried as she assured me everything would be okay.

I walked over to Harley's crib and peered past the tubes and wires into the face of my son. I whispered, "I love you," over and over again as I prayed. I realized that it was his due date – January 5th. Through months of carrying him, I never envisioned the day being filled with such sadness and pain.

As I pulled my hand back from his teddy-bear-covered hospital gown, it was as if I was releasing control of him. Through my intense pain and torrent of emotions, in that moment I somehow felt a sense of confidence that he would be okay. The slight improvements he had made over the last 24 hours assured me that he would soon recover. The dread in my heart pounded like the pain in my head, urging me to shift my focus to my own health.

My dad offered to drive me home. David stood at the door to greet me, his face flushed with fever. I'm sure my dad felt helpless as he deposited me on the couch. David's sickness left him in no real shape to take care of me. After a few hours of writhing at home, the pain became more than I could handle. I felt like I was dying. I called my oncologist to let her know that David was driving me to the ER. Despite a call from Dr. Miller to admit me, I had to endure hours in the emergency room before a space opened on the oncology floor.

David and I must have looked more than just disheveled when our friends, AngeLeah and Wes, came to see us in the early hours of the morning. "We're just a hot mess, huh?" AngeLeah's arm squeezed around my neck as she leaned over the rail jutting up the side of the bed, her tears splashing against my forehead. For the rest of the visit, they huddled close to the edge of the curtain – probably in an attempt to stay away from David's congestion-ridden germs. However, through the wee hours of the morning they did what only good friends can do; they made us laugh, they cried with us and they bore the silence when we didn't know what else to say.

The sun slanted through the blinds the next morning. The right side of my face pressed into the pillow as I lay in a bed on the oncology floor. The waffled pattern of the blanket etched a pattern on my arm as I tugged it around me to shield against the chill in the room. Squeaking shoes in the hallway became more frequent as the hospital awoke to a new day of tests and treatments.

For the past week, my role had been clearly defined as Harley's caregiver. Now I was flung back into life as a cancer patient.

I ran my finger along the rail of the bed until I found the button to lift my head. The pain medicine had kicked in enough to just take the edge off the torturous throbbing in my head. I trudged to the bathroom. I thought my eyes were just slow to adjust to the bright, florescent light in the cold, gray bathroom, but then I looked in the mirror. My eyelid sagged, covering half my eye. I could close it, but when I tried to open it fully, it wouldn't respond. I had cancer and my baby was still across town in the hospital, so adding cyclops to my list of maladies felt fitting.

During morning rounds, Dr. Miller noticed the change as well. "Due to the pressure the tumor is putting on your brain, your eye may continue to close. If it closes completely, it will probably never reopen." Awesome. The news just kept getting better.

The flurry of activity over the next few days did not leave much time to process the diagnosis or sift through our emotions.

David: *It felt like I was inside of a tornado. I still had a fever from bronchitis when Ashley was admitted to the hospital. My family didn't have time for me to be sick. Thankfully, Harley's condition began to improve, but he would still be in the hospital a few more days. I had to bounce back and forth between hospitals, always feeling like I needed to be in two places at one time.*

Working became almost an impossible task. Between being sick and taking care of my family, there were many days I called to tell my chief that there was just no way I could come to work. People began volunteering to work my shifts and donating their leave and sick days to me, without me even asking. The support I felt from my boss and my co-workers was incredible.

When I did manage to pull myself away, working a shift was almost a relief. I could pour my energy into tasks, just go through the motions. I didn't have as much down time to sit and think about the future. As much as I wanted to be with my wife and son, it broke my heart to watch them suffer, knowing there was nothing I could do to ease their pain.

Dr. Miller had consulted further with the doctor we had seen at Dana Farber in Boston. The urgency to begin treatment dramatically increased with the discovery of the brain tumor, yet the type of cancer still had not been determined, making treatment choices more complicated. The first step in the treatment process, radiation to my brain, would begin on Monday.

First, I had to be fitted for a radiation mask. During radiation treatments, radioactive lasers are fired to precise areas of the body. When radioactive lasers are involved, obviously, you need to be really still, so they anchor you down to the table with a space suit-type mask. The honeycomb pattern fit tightly against my face as they molded the exact specifications. Although I'm not typically a claustrophobic person, the process of being fitted for that radiation mask made me extremely uncomfortable. I felt like a caged animal.

Most of the weekend was spent managing my pain. As the intense pressure in my head and eye increased, I could almost picture the tumor growing. When oral medication could not bring relief, I was given pain patches. The patches were supposed to last 72 hours, but due to the severity of the pain, my doctor allowed me to change them every 48 hours.

My doctor also prescribed a steroid regimen. With any medication, there can be side effects, but with cancer treatments, the side effects are often pronounced. The effects of the steroids were noticeable almost immediately – ravenous appetite, trouble sleeping, irritability. My family probably noticed the irritability more quickly than I did though! The most noticeable side effect, however, was swelling. My body began to balloon, first my fingers and ankles, then my face and eventually my whole body. Tumor, sick baby, cyclops, marshmallow. Check.

Monday, January 8th

"Hi, I'm George. I'm here to take you to radiation." As he wheeled me across the breezeway, he made small talk, but not the kind that quickly becomes annoying. He seemed genuinely concerned about my situation and

151

talking to him helped quell my burgeoning level of anxiety. With my eye now fully closed and my peripheral vision limited to one side, I couldn't see my surroundings without constantly twisting my head from side to side. I tried to look at George as he talked, but gave up when shots of throbbing pain coursed through my head.

Patients dotted the drab blue and red chairs as George wheeled me next to the desk.

"We're ready for her. Bring her on back."

The sterile room felt like it should be on board a space ship. White cabinets and empty white counter tops wrapped around the right corner of the room, and a row of windows lined the left wall allowing the medical staff to observe the treatments. An enormous radiation machine rose up out of the squeaking tile floor in the center of the room. It looked like a giant microscope with the bed underneath the lens. It matched my sense of feeling like a science experiment.

I eased back onto the table and stared at the machine hanging above my head. A nurse brought out the mask I had been fitted for two days earlier. The honeycomb pattern pressed against my face as she fastened it down. As she worked, she talked me through the process.

"The most important thing to remember is to keep perfectly still." I wanted to assure her that the tightness of the mask made moving virtually impossible.

Wumpth.

The thick metal door sealed behind them. Sweat drops formed on my head, my hands felt sticky and my heart raced. This could not be good – the door was clearly designed to protect people from something, yet here I was *still inside the room.* Oh boy.

The machine roared to life. I prayed. I begged for protection from what seemed like a terrifying treatment and prayed that it would be effective. For so long I had been clawing and fighting to maintain control of my circumstances. I bulldozed anything in my path to protect my family and force the outcome I thought was best. For the past two months I had thrashed and flailed my way past round after round of bad news and uncertainty. Fear had replaced the driven, capable feeling that felt so familiar to me. Now, like a fish twisted tightly into a net, I had no power left to fight.

The physical forces pinning me to the table were weak compared to the fear that gripped my heart. The roller coaster of cancer had me firmly buckled into its front seat where there is no steering wheel or brake pedal. At the time it didn't occur to me that God may be trying to pry my fingers off the steering wheel of my life. I felt myself slipping toward fear and despair in my deepest thoughts. Maybe I could keep up appearance on the outside for the sake of my family and friends, but inside, my confidence was eroding.

Given the aggressive nature of the cancer, my doctor had prescribed the lifetime maximum level of radiation. I had prepared myself for the treatment to be intense, but I had not prepared for one thing – the smell. Over the next fifteen minutes I inhaled the effects of lasers burning through the flesh and brain matter in my skull. I would never be able to forget that smell.

I crumbled into my bed as George wheeled the chair out of the room. His gentle words, "Get some rest. I'll see you tomorrow," struck a new chord of fear in my heart. This would be my life five days a week for the next six weeks. I buried my head in the pillow and tried to forget. My mom walked over and rubbed my back, helpless to ease my pain.

David and his mom were at Scottish Rite Hospital where Harley was finally being discharged. While I felt disappointed that I couldn't be there, I was thankful that after eight days in the hospital, he would be going home. He would still need breathing treatments for several days, but thankfully Krista would be in town for a few days to help with those at home.

My mom and Patsy set up shifts to take care of Harley. My mom essentially moved into our house. She watched Harley during the day while Patsy watched him more at night and on the weekends since she still needed to teach school during the day. Control slipped further from my hands as I watched people take care of my family. They reluctantly stepped into my shoes. Our parents would have given anything for me to be the one at home taking care of Harley, but in my absence they were doing the best thing for him. I wondered if he would even remember me when we were finally reunited.

Just as he promised, George returned each morning that week. His kind words lifted my spirits each day on the way to and from radiation. After my fourth treatment on Thursday, my doctor had ordered a full-body CT scan with contrast. Since the cancer had already metastasized to my brain, it was necessary to make sure it had not spread further. The contrast dye would be injected into my veins, allowing the blood vessels to be illuminated. Cancer can usually be determined with this type of scan because a cancerous tumor needs a blood supply.

That afternoon Dr. Miller returned with the results. I rotated my head toward her, positioning myself to allow my left eye to focus on her slight frame. Her solemn eyes disclosed bad news before the words left her mouth.

"Ashley, your scans show that the cancer has metastasized further. The report states that there are innumerable tumors on your lungs and there is a small spot on your liver. It's stage four. Ashley, I'm so sorry."

She explained that there was no reason to biopsy anything else. Just like the tumor in my brain – they knew it was cancer. The glow on the CT scan was unmistakable.

Tears dropped from my cheeks and onto the blanket crumpled against my legs as I sat dumbfounded. This time, no uncontrolled emotional avalanche as before – just a silent stream of tears.

David: *Through my shock and disbelief, this diagnosis felt different. The first tumor felt manageable – surgery and it was done. With less than a week between finding out about the brain tumor to being told it was quickly consuming her body, it was like being punched in a boxing match before you even have a chance to get up. In a way though, I welcomed the news – not that the cancer had spread, but that aggressive treatments were beginning. I had been waiting for almost two months for treatments to begin, knowing the whole time that the cancer may be spreading. I was ready to go on offensive and stop just reacting to wave after wave of bad news.*

With the cancer spreading rampantly through my body, Dr. Miller explained the treatment plan going forward. My radiation treatments would be adjusted to include not only my brain tumor but also the area of my neck where the original tumor had been removed.

On Monday I would begin chemotherapy. While in the hospital, I would receive treatments weekly and then once every three weeks once I went home. The dosage had to be lower at first due to the radiation treatments, but once radiation was complete, I would receive the full dosage. She prescribed the chemotherapy drugs, Cisplatin and Taxol, designed for general head and neck cancers. Choosing which chemotherapy drugs to use proved difficult considering the type of cancer was still unknown. Given the rapid progression though, the type of cancer may not even matter. Time was not on our side.

Before chemo could begin, however, I would need surgery for a port to be placed in my upper right chest. The port would be used to administer chemotherapy and other medications and could also be used for drawing blood. On Friday morning, I kissed David as they wheeled me to the operating room. Our moms waited with him, for what we were told would be a quick, one-hour surgery, while my dad and Krista stayed at home with Harley. My arms ached to hold him again.

David: *Two hours into the surgery, we grew concerned about what was going on. It felt like a replay of the tumor surgery. What could be going wrong? We were told this would be simple. After three hours, the surgeon came out to explain that while the port is typically placed on the right, a complication with Ashley's vein structure forced her to have to move the port to the left side. Could nothing be easy?*

Not only did our family step up to support us, our church family and friends rallied around us as well. Our friends, Wes & AngeLeah, provided a housecleaner, alleviating that burden from David and our moms. Meals began showing up at our house when Harley came home from the hospital. Southerners are always great at feeding people, but especially in times of crisis. It's like we don't know what else to do, so we just make food. Food baskets were delivered to the hospital with snacks and drinks for me and my visitors. People brought food almost daily to

157

feed David and whoever was at the house helping with Harley. The oncology floor had a community kitchen, and David would often bring leftovers from home to keep at the hospital. However, David secretly loved hospital food, especially the chicken fingers!

I, on the other hand, struggled to eat anything. Despite being hungry, the effects of the radiation on my throat made eating painful. I learned that cold things felt good on my throat, but unfortunately nothing cold and healthy appealed to me. Jell-O, ice cream, pudding, pie, and smoothies soothed my burning throat. In moments of self-pity, they soothed my spirit as well. If I had cancer, why not eat what I wanted to?

I developed a love for Starbucks Frappuccinos. Okay, an obsession. Visitors learned about my sudden obsession and would bring a Frappuccino often. My doctor had informed me that during chemo and radiation, it was important not to lose weight. So, my daily Frappuccino just helped me do my part.

Sunday night, my parents surprised me and brought Harley for a visit. Nothing could have lifted my spirits more than seeing my precious boy. He certainly looked healthier than when I had left him nine days earlier. The relentless aching in my head made it difficult for me to look down at him, so I pulled him close against my chest and leaned my head back, pressing my eyes closed. His little heart beating against mine renewed my strength to fight through the pain and treatments.

Monday, January 15

Chemotherapy is an all-day event. I knew people that had had cancer and had received chemo. I didn't realize the multiple steps and long hours involved. The blood work, pre-meds, and treatments took nearly five hours. I curled up in the chair as the nurse prepared my port for the medicine.

"You're lucky they accessed your port for the first time during your surgery. It is really painful the first time!" I managed a weak smile. I clutched the iPod, pressed play, and closed my eye. A cool sensation coursed down my chest as the medicine began to flow.

"I'll be back to check on you in a bit."

Even though my pain patches had just been changed the night before, my head throbbed like a bass drum. Nothing brought relief. I struggled to sit still during the treatment, desperate to find a position to relieve the pain. David sat with me, keeping me company even though I knew I was pretty boring company for him. He lovingly encouraged me, told me stories about Harley, and tried to make me laugh.

A few days later, after two weeks in a hospital bed and multiple daily treatments, I longed for something to keep my mind busy. In the fall I had been in charge of organizing our church's couples' retreat. It would be in late January. My parents agreed to come with us to watch Harley. My anticipation grew as details came together. I looked forward to a weekend in the mountains with friends, our new son, and built-in babysitters. The deposits were made and everything seemed ready to go.

After my diagnosis, I knew we would not be able to go and informed the couples at church. The sadness surrounding my diagnosis was thick and everyone agreed it would be best to cancel the trip. I called the lodge to inform them of the situation and they promptly refunded the deposit. All that was left to do was to write checks back to each couple who had paid. My mom offered to write the checks for me and assured me that no one would care if I waited a few weeks to return their money. In fact, she told me some people would rather me just keep the money to use for our family's expenses.

No, I insisted it be done and insisted that I would be the one to do it. Once again, it was something tangible that I could control and manage. I was determined to write the checks despite my severe pain, medications, and one eye out of commission. My mom relented and brought me my checkbook and the list of names. Over the next hour I confidently wrote the checks as if nothing were wrong and handed them back to my mom.

At church the following Sunday, my mom couldn't help but chuckle as she passed out the checks. They looked like they had been written by a preschooler.

In my determination, I couldn't even see how poor my handwriting had become. When I realized later how awful the checks looked, I couldn't help but laugh.

Chapter 14
Frappuccinos for Life

"Let us therefore come boldly unto the throne of grace, that we may obtain mercy, and find grace to help in time of need." Heb. 4:16

Just home from the hospital, I curled up in a new recliner, which had become my favorite spot in the house. It allowed me to feel a part of the family, even when I couldn't be up and moving around. It had been donated to us by Community Bank of West Georgia where I had worked during college. Even though I was physically present, the high doses of pain medication kept me far away from everyone in every other way. I lived in a fog most days – a blob of humanity that could barely carry on coherent conversations or get up for anything other than to use the bathroom or go to the doctor.

Our moms continued their day and night schedule taking care of Harley. My brother, Joshua, helped organized fundraisers to help pay for our medical expenses. Our dads, Krista, and Nathan helped as they could while continuing to work full time jobs. Our church continued to support us through meals, donations, prayers, and visits when I felt up to having company. I was in awe of how many people had surrounded us. It was staggering.

David's words rattled me from my thoughts. "Ashley, it's time to go." I sat up, reluctant to put Harley down. David helped me out of the chair after passing Harley off to my mom. Despite having been home for only a few days, the daily trips to the hospital for radiation already felt routine. As I pulled my seatbelt across my chest, I winced as it brushed my neck. Redness extended along my jawline and down my throat. It looked as if I had fallen asleep on the beach with my head turned to one side. I pulled a gel wrap out of my purse and draped it against my neck to help soothe the burning.

Sores had developed in my mouth and down my throat, making eating and drinking even more painful, if that were possible. And I was hot – always hot. It felt like a fire burned from the inside out. David, my mom, and Patsy learned to bundle up in the house because I frequently kept the heat and the fireplace off. The rapid avalanche of side effects overwhelmed me. Every day it was something new. But honestly, what did I expect? Radioactive lasers were being fired into my neck and brain in an attempt to kill a stage-four, non-operable, death-sentence cancer that was spreading like wild fire in my body. Mild side effects were outside the realm of possibility.

I smiled as I saw the pink baseball cap across the waiting room. Since radiation treatments are scheduled at the same time each day, five days a week, for normally 6-8 weeks, you see the same people in the waiting room each time. Janet and I shared the same treatment schedule and developed a friendship after just a few days. If I were a glass-half empty, sarcastic, "Well, if I'm going to die, I might as well drink Frappuccinos on the way out" kind of person, Janet was my opposite. Her positive outlook radiated through her face, words, actions, and attitude. Her greetings bubbled up from a heart full of gratitude and love.

After talking to Janet, you would think that she had something simple, like a sinus infection, not cancer. Her positive outlook was contagious. I enjoyed talking with her and could easily forget my plight during our conversations. Her smile exploded one day when she found out our son's name was Harley.

"How sweet! My baby is a Harley too!" She was a self-proclaimed biker chick and loved all things Harley Davidson. She started showing up to treatments with Harley Davidson gear for Harley: onesies, a little jacket, socks, and hats. I could easily picture her riding her bike, red fingernails gripping the controls, her red hair blowing in the wind as her infectious laugh filled the air around her.

Before we parted each day, Janet would assure me that she would pray for me. I would return the thought, but I felt like she was on the losing end of that deal. Between the pain and sleepless nights, fear would creep into my thoughts, invading my prayers like the cancer that was invading my body. Janet's calm centeredness testified of a firm foundation in her faith. While I sometimes felt like I had to dig through layers of shifting sand, past my grasping for control and questioning God to hit the same

163

bedrock of faith. I was humbled that she would think to pray for me. She had every right to spend all of her efforts praying for herself, but her example nudged my heart to take my eyes off myself and my circumstances long enough to pray for those around me.

Sheila: *At radiation the next day, I followed my normal routine. As the light above the large metal door would flick on, I would start to pray. I would sit in silent prayer until the light went off. However, on that day I had an interruption. Janet's sister slid into the seat across from me. Like her sister, she immediately encouraged me with her smile and warm attitude.*

"Janet's prognosis is not good. The doctors only give her a few months." She patted the corner of her eye with a tissue as she continued. "You would never know it talking to Janet though. Her attitude is contagious. If she believes she can beat this, we do too."

While I had an amazing church family and friends, few people understood the burden that we carried. To share stories and prayers with someone who understood, even for just a few minutes, felt like such a relief. We each reached for fresh tissues. I knew the light would turn off soon and I didn't want to be a blubbery mess when Ashley came out. After that day, we shared a hug each time saw each other.

On the way home, my mom shared Janet's prognosis with me. I dismissed the thought.

164

"Janet will beat this. If anyone can, she can. She seems like she's doing well." Considering my own grim prognosis, I couldn't allow my thoughts to go down the path of statistics and facts.

Sunday, January 27

It had been weeks since we had been to church as a family, but I was determined that today we would be there. We had to be there. Harley's baby dedication would be held during the evening service. With all day to get ready, I shouldn't have been running late. My swollen body moved at a snail's pace, frustrating my fast-paced thoughts. The steroid regimen had taken a massive toll on my body. Whatever good they were doing on the inside, didn't seem worth it on the outside. The two main side effects – swelling and increased appetite – were not a good combination for a postpartum mom whose workout regimen consisted of getting lasered with radioactive toxins on a daily basis.

Sitting in my hospital bed for two weeks and receiving chemo and radiation treatments in an attempt to save my life, I hadn't thought too much about nutrition or the numbers on the scale. In addition to my daily Frappuccinos, people frequently brought me soft, cold foods that would soothe my fiery throat, none of which were healthy.

One evening Krista's parents, Billy and Shirley, brought me my favorite dessert from a local Italian restaurant: white chocolate raspberry cheesecake. The large pieces should be shared, but when David's fork attempted to cross paths with mine, I snapped, "Get your own piece. I have cancer." He chuckled, but despite my smirk, he realized I was serious. I enjoyed the whole piece.

Pajamas, yoga pants, and t-shirts were my uniform on most days. Toward the end of my hospital stay, I had noticed that even those forgiving waistbands had become snug. David offered to go to Target to buy me some clothes. Without even being asked, Krista grabbed her purse to go with him.

Krista: *I was afraid David would be overwhelmed in the women's clothing section at Target. For a man that wears uniforms to work, I thought he could use some help with styles and sizes. It was one of the few times we had been alone since Ashley's diagnosis.*

"David, you know God may take Ashley, right? I know we need to be positive for her and God can do anything, but you know how bad it is, right?" The nurse inside me screamed that this was not going to end well.

Keeping his eyes on the road he said, "I know. I know He could take her. I'm just gonna' keep praying for His will. I guess that's all we can do."

They came back with bulging red and white bags hanging from their arms. Nothing fit. When they had to return all the clothes for a bigger size, I realized how much my body had changed in just a few weeks. I was shocked.

Those changes made finding a dress for the baby dedication unbearable. I glared at the dress draped across the end of the bed, the tags still attached. I had to put it on. I had to go. I didn't know how much longer I had to live or what kind of quality of life I would be facing in my uncertain future. Harley may look back on these pictures one day and see a mom who died before he was old enough to know her. If that were the case, I wanted him to know that he had a mom who loved him, prayed for him, and dedicated his life to the Lord. No dress would stand between me and that mission.

If I can keep this on through the service, no one will have to see my dress, I muttered to myself as I pulled the buttons closed on the long black coat I had purchased the day before. With my immune system almost non-existent due to the chemo and radiation treatments, going into a crowd of hand-shaking, hugging church people at the height of flu season felt precarious, but it was a necessary risk given the circumstances. I added a mask and gloves to my already uncomfortable outfit. David shielded me from people as we walked in the back door. Being our first service back since news of the brain cancer, our friends were eager to greet us. My family and our pastor helped tell people to keep their distance. I felt more like a science experiment than a jubilant new mom.

Our family squeezed together on the pew in the front of the long, narrow sanctuary. As our pastor, Brother Eddie, preached a message about being godly parents, I wondered if I would be around long enough to implement any of what he said. Harley squirmed as we eased out of the pew and walked toward the front of the church. Each family participating knelt down at the altar for a time of prayer, followed by a Bible presentation to each child. I blotted my tears with tissues as we knelt. My right eye still leaked tears despite its failure to open and be of any use.

David: *Everything had been such a whirlwind surrounding Harley's birth. I knew I was a dad, but praying at the altar that night, I felt the weight of what it meant to be a parent. I desperately wanted to be a good dad to Harley and raise him to love the Lord. Simultaneously, I bore the weight of the possibility that I may have to be a single parent to this little guy. Knowing Ashley's body was riddled with so much pain and disease, I wanted to take it from her. I wanted to be a family and raise our son together. I begged God for His mercy to heal her as much as I had prayed for anything in my life.*

***

It seemed fitting that Groundhog's Day fell the next week. It felt like days were on repeat. Daily trips to radiation consumed most of our time. Someone had to go with me, and someone had to stay with Harley while everyone else tried to work. The sores in my mouth grew worse, making eating more difficult each day.

One day after radiation, my mom and I went through the Starbuck's drive-thru on our way home. My favorite part of the Frappuccinos was the whipped cream.

168

The billowy white cream numbed the burning sores on my throat unlike anything else I could drink. I craved the soothing effect.

Pulling up to the box, I ordered my mom's drink and then mine.

"Could I get a grande caramel Frappuccino in a venti cup so you have room to put some extra whipped cream?" The long sigh I received in response caught me off guard.

"Ma'am, are you sure you want extra whipped cream?"

"Yes, please," I responded, assuming the barista was simply ensuring he got the order correct.

"Well, ma'am," the voice snapped, "the amount normally included is generous already. Are you sure you need extra?"

"Yes, please," I answered, now annoyed. I jerked the car around the building to the window, thinking there would be no response. Who would argue with a dying cancer patient's guilty pleasure? But at the window, the barrage continued. A tall, lanky guy turned toward the window, holding our drinks in his hands. His black finger nails matched his hair and his ear lobes were the size of quarters thanks to expanders.

"You do realize whipped cream is unhealthy for you, right?"

"Well, actually, I have cancer and probably don't have very long to live. I just finished a radiation treatment and that whipped cream is the only thing that helps me

169

through, so I'll take the extra whipped cream," I retorted. My response only fueled his disgust.

"That's all the more reason you shouldn't be drinking it! Ma'am, do you realize the effect sugar has on cancer? Sugar is the fuel that feeds cancer. If you have cancer, you really shouldn't be drinking these at all. Do you know what this whipped cream does when we pour it in the sink?"

I blinked repeatedly to keep tears from splashing down my cheeks, my jaw hanging open as I struggled to comprehend what was happening. Was he seriously arguing with me over my choice of beverage and judging my decisions?

"Sir, I have no idea what whipped cream does in your sink. I can't say that I've ever put whipped cream down a drain." My voice trailed off. I typically do not struggle to find words during conflict, but his response left me speechless. My mom rested her hand gently on my hand, bringing me back to reality.

"Could I just have my drinks please?" I snapped, thrusting my credit card toward the window.

Sheila: *I wouldn't typically describe Ashley as a laid-back, go-with-the-flow kind of gal. She's always been driven, smart, and organized; however, the pain medication seemed to accentuate the more determined side of her personality. Her temper was a bit quicker and fuse a bit shorter some days. Knowing the amount of medication she was on, we knew a lot of what she said and did wasn't her*

– it was the medication. I would just pat her gently on the arm sometimes to just reassure her that everything was going to be okay. And I tried to not make eye contact with the barista.

I paid and shoved the gas pedal down as we pulled out of the parking lot. At home, I gathered my thoughts enough to form my response into words, called the store, and asked to speak to the manager. I received gift cards and an apology from the manager, which simply meant more whipped cream for me. I'm sure the nutrition-conscience barista would have been horrified.

February 6, 2008

I grabbed a butterscotch as I walked by the receptionist's desk. I popped it in my mouth and let the smooth, buttery candy run down, soothing my blister lined throat. David walked behind me as we snaked around the chairs in the infusion room toward the exam rooms lining the back wall. The marathon chemo day had arrived. My neck burned from radiation just a few hours before, and now I was about to assault my body with a round of chemo. Dr. Miller greeted David and me in the exam room. Her upbeat spirit was shrouded with a sense of urgency and concern. With the cancer multiplying so rapidly, none of us knew if the treatments would have time to work.

As she recorded the orders for the day and left the room I breathed a prayer over her. "Jesus help her," was

171

all I could muster at the time, but it felt like enough. I imagined that she carried a tremendous burden. As an oncologist, every day she faced people teetering between life and death, each one placing his or her confidence in Dr. Miller's expertise. I prayed that God would give her the wisdom to fight this unknown, ferocious cancer exploding in my cells.

Next, the nurse drew blood for the routine, pre-chemo lab tests. If my white blood cell count was too low or anything else was off in my blood work, the treatment would be canceled. Building up the anticipation of chemo day, only to have to go back home due to something off in my blood work assaulted my nerves. Thankfully, the nurse reported a few minutes later that my numbers looked good. What a relief.

The infusion room looked like a drab donut made out of medical recliners. Each patient chair had a companion chair, with tables scattered throughout the room. A massive aquarium filled half the far wall. I wilted into the chair, already drowsy from the antihistamine, which was part of a fist full of premeds I had just taken.

Through the tops of the chairs, I peered into a small side room, which was nothing more than a small box with a counter and a window. A burly guy in a white lab coat looked more like a scientist than a lab tech as he mixed the elixirs of chemotherapy drugs together as he received orders. His work intrigued me. I'm not sure I would have wanted that job – mixing powerful chemicals designed to kill living cells. Not really stuff you want to spill or splatter.

David headed to the stocked mini-fridge and snack cabinet while we waited. Props of being a cancer patient – free snacks and drinks while you wait! He came back with a Strawberry Kiwi Propel for me and a Coke and bag of chips for himself.

My friend, Melissa, walked over to begin my infusion. Melissa and I had met through a mutual friend at church back in high school. Seeing a familiar face during treatments made the process less daunting. During my hospital stay, Melissa would frequently stop by on her way to work to share a biscuit and a laugh. Sometimes, I just needed someone around who wasn't weepy and overwhelmed by the thought of cancer, chemotherapy, and radiation. Someone on the outside enough not to be as emotionally attached, but connected enough to shoot straight with me about my condition and prognosis.

Another friend from high school, also named Melissa (thank you 1980's…), worked as an infusion nurse as well. In high school, Melissa Walker and I had worked together on a project about The Black Death in Europe during the 1300's. The irony was not lost.

Melissa accessed my port, and I closed my eyes as the medicine flowed into my body. Once I fell asleep, David took lunch orders from the Melissas and the rest of the nurses. In the South, Chick-fil-a is always the lunch of choice. Seriously, we eat Chick-fil-a enough for the rest of the country. A number one – a classic chicken sandwich with fries and a sweet tea or lemonade – should be a food group below the Mason Dixon line. Occasionally he would get Mexican or Subway, but not often.

He returned an hour later, laden with red and white foam cups and two large plastic bags adorned with the red and white chicken logo. When I woke up, he presented me with a yogurt parfait. Chicken, French fries, or salads would have been impossible to swallow due to the sores on my throat. Even chicken soup wasn't an option since it would have magnified the constant burning feeling. I pushed my glasses on and pressed on the arm rest to sit up. I took a few bites before handing it back. Inevitably, I knew whatever went down would probably come back up after chemo.

I listened to my iPod as I grew restless waiting for the treatment to end. My mom texted me a picture of Harley. Holding him eased the sickness and pain in my body as well as my heart. Despite being distracted with appointments and therapies, I watched as he sprouted from a sleepy newborn to an alert three-month old infant. His grin and giggles lit up a room. On one hand, I was thankful he was too young to remember anything going on around him, but on the other, if I didn't make it, he would be too young to remember me. I couldn't do the normal things a mother should do for her baby, but I could hold him. I would prop my arm up, and he and I would sleep together, often in the recliner. I just wanted to go home.

The sun hung low in the sky as we walked to the car. David helped me into the seat, my body weak despite sitting in a chair all day. Snuggled with Harley in the recliner at home that evening, I listened to Harley's rhythmic breathing in my ear as the only sound in the room. Then something tapped at the door. Family and friends knew not to ring the doorbell or knock loudly. Both would send Lulu into a barking frenzy. Any loud noises were amplified in my head, so everyone tried to create a quiet environment, especially on my darker days.

My dad walked in, a slight grin on his face. He placed a brown paper bag on the kitchen table. From my perch in the living room, I watched him pull out two giant Starbucks cups. My dad's trademark is his tender heart. If he discovers you like something, bank on my dad getting it for you. He had heard about my run in with the Starbucks barista and wanted to surprise me after a long day at chemo. He presented me with the two cups. My first thought was, "Wow, now that is extra whipped cream on a Frappuccino!" but I soon realized the cups were filled with nothing *but* whipped cream.

My mom wedged a cup in my opposite hand as I still held Harley, a plastic green spoon balanced on top. For a moment I felt guilty, but the feelings washed away as the velvety goodness filled my mouth. I chuckled as I thought about what the health-nut barista would say to me now, but figured if cancer was going to take me down, my hips wouldn't mind a little extra padding on the way.

Chapter 15
Battle over Bottles

"Many are the afflictions of the righteous;
but the Lord delivereth them out of them all." Ps. 34:19

The MRI machine hummed around me. I found myself holding my breath trying not to move as the white tube engulfed me. The mind-numbing pain still relentless in my head made it difficult to stay perfectly still. Dr. Miller hoped these images, along with the CT I had just received, would show some improvements, some indication that the treatments were working. Isaiah 41:10 rang through my head:

Fear thou not; for I am with thee: be not dismayed; for I am thy God: I will strengthen thee; yea, I will help thee; yea, I will uphold thee with the right hand of my righteousness.

Fear not. Fear not. I'm no Bible scholar, but I tried to put in context those words. The Bible doesn't exactly have a chapter and verse for people fighting cancer. Death loomed as a real possibility, yet these words "Fear not" applied to me as much as they did the Israelites when Isaiah wrote them. They were surrounded by captors on every side, yet God told them not to be afraid because He was with them. I clung to that hope. He was with me – no matter what these scans showed.

As I let the air inch out of my lungs, I tried to push my thoughts far away from the hospital, tests, and doctors. They drifted to David. He had been a rock over the last several months as our lives had been flipped upside down. Even in moments when my emotions whirled, he remained calm, never resorting to panic or hysteria. He had always been that way.

Like most couples, our first year of marriage wasn't always sunshine and roses, although David remembers it as exactly that. When I talk about our early days, David jokes that we must have been living in two different houses. Apparently he remembers more gazing into each other's eyes than I do. I remember discussions about squeezing the toothpaste the correct way and making a budget and actually sticking to it. David's carefree, positive attitude stood in stark contrast to my more realistic, practical view. I tend to see the glass half empty, but David's glass is *always* half full.

I needed his optimism now more than ever. The marathon day that had begun with radiation, followed by the CT, MRI, and then chemo mirrored many of my days. My body was growing weary along with my resolve. I didn't know how much more my body could handle.

February 10

Two days later, Harley and I assumed our position in the recliner. The chemo had taken its toll on me. I had spent the morning upstairs crawling back and forth to the bathroom if I needed to throw up. The leprosy-like sores in my mouth and throat hurt constantly, especially when I attempted to swallow anything other than whipped cream. They *really* hurt when the contents of my stomach came back up, assaulting them along the way.

The day after each chemo treatment I had to return to the doctor's office to receive two shots. One hurt terribly to get, which was to boost my white blood cell count and help keep me from developing infections. The next one, designed to increase my red blood cell count, didn't hurt to get, but it seemed to cause more harm than good. In the days following the shot, my bones felt like they were breaking from the inside out. I couldn't stand. I was forced to crawl or slither on the ground to get back and forth to the bathroom. The thought of going up or down the stairs seemed so daunting that I only attempted it if absolutely necessary. Since there was no bathroom on the main floor, I stayed upstairs most of the time on really bad days.

When the nausea relented, I had inched my way down the stairs toward the recliner. I sipped a strawberry Propel to try to ease the searing pain in my throat and the churning in my stomach. Harley's face wrinkled as he stretched his arms and legs simultaneously, his body beginning to wake up. His eyes blinked and met mine for the first time that day. His lips smacked in anticipation of something to eat. My mom brought me a bottle, propping it against my chin so neither one of us had to move. This little guy had no idea what it was like to need something. With grandparents around 24/7, his needs were anticipated before he had a chance to cry. "Saddle up buddy," I thought. "When Mommy gets better, you may actually have to cry sometimes. Oh, and you may not be held all the time either. Mommy didn't used to lie around like this all the time. Just letting you know, so you're prepared."

When he finished eating, my mom scooped him up, draped him over her shoulder, and patted his back gently as she swayed.

"Ashley look," she gasped. A clump of hair covered his tiny fist. He had pulled a chunk of hair out of my head and I hadn't even noticed. I hadn't even felt it. My hair had been coming out more and more with each passing day. David and our moms were constantly sweeping and vacuuming. It clogged the shower drain and lined my pillow every morning. Brushing my hair would produce ponytail sized clumps in my brush. Sections on the back of my head were bald already.

David stuck his head around from inside the kitchen. Our eyes locked.

"It's time," I sighed, breathing out the frustration seething under my skin. I crawled upstairs as David pulled a chair into our bathroom. He draped a sheet around me, his eyes never raising to meet mine as his sock feet shuffled along the bathroom floor.

"No," I snapped. "If we are going to do this, let's have some fun. We knew this would happen. Let's not make it a cry fest."

179

My mom laid Harley on a blanket and grabbed the camera. David pulled out the clippers. He cut his own hair, so I guess that made him the only qualified barber in the house. Then again, how could you mess up this kind of hair cut?

My shoulder length brown hair tumbled to the ground as he made the first pass around my left ear. My mom snapped pictures as he cut, the clippers zipping around like a lawnmower on an overgrown lawn. He sculpted a mohawk at first. After a few more pictures, and realizing I didn't want to be known at radiation treatments as "the girl with the mohawk," he shaved the rest. The clippers left my head a ball of brown fuzz, like a six-year-old boy's haircut.

I felt disgusted. Cancer had taken my freedom, my health, my time, and now my hair. I probably should have thought about things like "true beauty comes from within" or "God doesn't look on the outward appearance," but in that moment all I could think was, "I look like a freak show." I felt disgusting and ugly. I couldn't leave it like this. I couldn't stand the fuzz.

David brought me my razor out of the shower. You know the girls that can shave their legs once a week (*or less*) during the winter? I'm just not one of those girls. I shave my legs every day, even when I'm *actually* dying. I cannot stand the feel of stubble or fuzz on my body. Nope, the fur ball could not stay on my head. If I had to lose my hair, I at least wanted it to feel smooth.

We carefully shaved my head, David helping with the back and around my ears. Afterwards, I showered and crawled back to bed, exhausted from the ordeal. In the shower as I went to shave my legs, I only had a few small patches of stubble. Second bonus of having cancer (the first was obviously the Frappuccinos) – not having to shave my legs or my armpits. I had never considered that *all* of my hair would fall out. That was one side effect I could deal with!

February 12

I screwed my eyes tightly shut trying to block out the florescent glow of the light above me. I knew it would probably be hours before a bed opened up on the oncology floor. The ER doctor had been able to do little to alleviate the pain from the sores lining my mouth and my throat. Despite the amount of medication through the patches on my back, the pain from the sores had been too much to endure at home. They were like volcanoes erupting along my gum line, cheeks, and down my throat.

Dr. Miller came into the room after I had been moved to the oncology floor. The bad news lined her face. The silence hung in the air like damp clothes pinned to the line on a windless, summer day as she flipped the chart.

"Unfortunately, the CT results show that some of the masses on your lungs have grown in size."

Her words punched a hole through my feeble optimism. The treatments weren't working. The treatments that were stealing my strength and well-being.

The treatments that were taking me away from my son and dominating my time. They weren't working. My thoughts seethed toward cancer and chemotherapy and pain patches and radiation. What was the point? *I was dying anyway!*

"What about the MRI? Has the brain tumor grown?" I stammered, pushing the words out with air in my cancer-ridden lungs.

"The MRI report will take longer to get back. The radiologist noted that he needs to compare it to the previous MRI."

Silence fell again. Her shoulders slumped slightly as she exhaled. If her thoughts mirrored her body language, she was on the cusp of giving up. How many times had she given this news to patients? I imagined she could see what my coming days would look like, as she had seen it so many times before.

After that day, my thoughts shifted. I didn't lose my will to live, but I let reality sink further into my soul.

I was probably going to die.

I couldn't ignore the pressing weight of evidence that the cancer was spreading too fast to be stopped. The more time I spent on the oncology floor, the deeper my relationships grew with the nurses and staff. They helped me understand my options, given the news.

"You know you don't have to continue treatments. If you decide you want to stop, it's okay. The treatments are robbing you of precious time with your husband, son, and family. If you want to stop and go home and enjoy your final days, it's okay."

For a moment I wondered if the pain and suffering caused by the treatments were worth it. If the cancer wouldn't respond to treatments, maybe I would be better off spending what time I had left with Harley and David far away from hospitals and treatment rooms. My family wouldn't have to watch me suffer anymore. I could regain my strength and end the pain caused by the sores and shots. I may even feel pretty good for a little while. We could drive to the beach and drink in the beauty of a sunset together.

As my mind trailed further down what felt like the easier road, I snatched my thoughts back from the chasm of despair.

"No," I responded, clenching my fists. "I want to fight this. I'll do whatever it takes." I knew death was almost certain, but I could not give up. David deserved more. Harley deserved more. My family and friends deserved it. They made the pain of the treatment worth something. As David recounted my story to Harley one day, I wanted him to be able to say that I gave it all I had – that I didn't give up. I never wanted Harley to wonder why I stopped treatment, and I wanted him to have the assurance that his mom left nothing on the table in her fight against the cancer that took her away from him.

While Dr. Miller understood my resolve to continue treatments, she chose to pause my radiation treatments due to the severity of the sores in my mouth and throat. She prescribed a round of antibiotics in order to clear up any possible infection associated with the sores. Food became even less appealing as the ooze from the sores distorted the taste. My tongue felt like a roll of paper towels lodged between my teeth, relentlessly sticking the roof of my mouth and the scabs crowding my cheeks.

Adding to my discomfort, my right ear started hurting, going from a dull ache to a mind-numbing throb, like a drum pounding against my brain tumor. Dr. Parks stopped by my room to take a look. He informed me that fluid had built up behind my right ear drum, a common side effect of radiation to the head. The next day, Valentine's Day, as I was wheeled back into surgery to have a tube inserted to drain the fluid from ear, I felt like a voodoo doll being pierced over and over and over again.

Later that evening, the door cracked open. I tilted my head to bring the door into view with my only working eye. My mom peeked in at first and then pushed the door slightly, allowing room for my dad to file in, Harley's car seat dangling from his arm. I mustered a smile as I saw Harley's feet resting on the edge of the seat, his Valentine's outfit visible between the straps.

Harley's visit that night brightened my mood temporarily, but that too brought sadness. As my mom wedged him between my arm and my chest we posed for a picture, I wondered if he even knew me. I could have just as easily been a beanbag chair that supported him rather than his mom. My mom, David's mom, and even Krista were with him far more than me. I wanted to jump up, rip the port from my chest, and march out of the room, leaving my cancer behind on the bed. If things could have only been that easy.

A few minutes later, Brother Eddie walked in, joining the impromptu Valentine's celebration. On this visit I had been lucky enough to get a large room on the oncology floor, providing enough space for everyone to visit comfortably. I imagined the conversations at the nurses' station when they heard I was being admitted: "Ashley Hallford is coming in." "Oh no, the big room hasn't been cleaned!" "Well, we better get someone on that – you know the crowd of people they have!"

I struggled to participate in the conversation; my raspy voice and my raw throat made speaking difficult. Knowing I had chemo the next day, everyone left early, giving me time to rest. As I kissed Harley good night, I felt sure I would not be around to see his next Valentine's Day.

Patsy: *Sheila and I continued to work together to take care of Harley while Ashley was in the hospital. He was such a little ray of sunshine for all of us. Taking care of him was a breeze compared to taking care of Lulu. If it had been up to me, Lulu would have found a new home during those months! She always seemed to complicate an already difficult situation. One particular day, Sheila and I walked in and found the playroom covered in poop. I wished for a nanny camera in that room so I could see how she managed to make such a mess! In our fit of anger at the* pup while cleaning up the room with plastic gloves up to our elbows, we gave Lulu quite the lecture.

Thankfully David didn't have to deal with that mess on his own. Poor David. He never uttered a disgruntled word or complaint, but I could see the stress weighing on him. It was like he had lost his wife. The pain medications and steroids morphed her personality into an almost unrecognizable state at times. All of her physical strength was taken by the cancer and treatments. Her mind was foggy and moods unpredictable. Her normal wit and humor disappeared under a layer of bitterness and sadness.

No one prepares you for any of that when your wife is diagnosed with cancer. We struggled to know how to comfort and help our son. When Ashley and David were dating, I walked into his room and sat down on the edge of the bed. I could tell things were moving toward marriage, and like any mom would, I wanted him to be sure she was the right girl. I asked, "Do you really love her? Marriage is for better or worse, David. It's in sickness and in health, no matter what happens." Those words echoed in my mind. I knew David loved Ashley and would do anything for her. He would have, but there's no handbook for navigating such difficult circumstances.

I could see a resentment in Ashley building toward anyone taking care of Harley, especially toward Sheila and me. Every first-time mom is picky about how her child is cared for, that's expected. Given Ashley's personality, that is probably even a little more so, but beneath the feeding schedule and sleeping regimen, I sensed a seething anger. Ashley was clawing for control. She wanted to be the one taking care of Harley. While we all knew she was grateful for the help, the pain, the medication, and the ominous reports all took their toll.

At home, between hospital stays, things seemed to reach a boiling point. Normally Sheila and I would relieve each other, switching shifts in the early evening. However, if Ashley was having a really bad day, then we would both stay. Around 2:00AM, we were still up, having just finished feeding Harley. Sheila took the bottle into the kitchen to wash it while I sat on the couch with Harley. (He needed to be held upright for 20 minutes after every feeding to help with his acid reflux.)

Suddenly Ashley appeared, stomping down the stairs. As she marched across the living room and into the kitchen, I stood, following silently behind. Ashley stood hip to hip at the sink with her mom. She reached for the bottle and brush, yanking it from her mom's hands.

"I need to show y'all how to wash these bottles," she snapped. She plunged the brush in the bottle, pumping it furiously until suds poured over the edge of the bottle. She pushed the bottle under the running water and flung it on the drying rack. She proceeded to give a lecture on how to reassemble the bottle when it was dry, as if we hadn't been doing the exact same process for months.

"And that's how you wash a bottle." She spun around and stormed back upstairs. Sheila and I stood stunned as she exited, knowing we had just witnessed a *rage of steroids and medication at work.   When she was safely out of ear shot, we both let out a batch of giggles.*

"Well, I guess we just got a good course on bottle washing," Sheila chuckled, turning back to the sink.

Chapter 16
To the New Mrs. Hallford

"From the end of the earth will I cry unto thee, when my heart is
overwhelmed;
lead me to the rock that is higher than I." Ps. 61:2

At my elementary school's fall festival each year, my favorite booth stood at the end. The blue board had two cut out circles. You were handed a fishing pole with a clothespin dangling at the end. Knowing what lay on the other side, the choice was simple. If you stuck your pole in the first hole, you would pull out a small bag of cheap candy – a boring prize in the midst of caramel apples, cotton candy and funnel cakes. Through the other hole lay a greater prize. Much to my parents' dismay, what came through the hole, snuggly fastened to the wooden clothespin, stirred joy in my heart. The bag gleamed in the warm fall sunshine, bulging as I ripped it from its hook. A tiny orange gold fish floated in its watery home. I couldn't wait to get it home. I just knew it would be a lifelong pet.

If you've ever had fish, you know my dreams were quickly dashed. The fish only lived a few days, probably traumatized from my enthusiastic jostling throughout the rest of the fall festival. I watched for two days as the little fish struggled. On his final day, he lay at the bottom of the tank, his little gills bursting with every breath. He was dying. My mom finally took him out of my room so I didn't have to watch him suffer anymore. Appropriately, his name was Goldie.

I felt like Goldie lying on the bottom of the fish tank while my family watched me suffer. I stared back at them from the bottom. In my helpless state I watched as everyone lived my life around me. Not their lives. My mom's life had stopped. She and Patsy filled the role of Harley's mom much more than I did. They did everything I couldn't do. I hated it. Guilt and resentment mirrored each other in my soul. Our families were laying aside their lives to take care of us; how could I feel resentful? Cancer and the medication had taken the best part of me and left only a skeleton of my former self. The once independent, determined person was now a helpless, bald carcass that couldn't care for herself, let alone her family.

I spent more time in the hospital than out. The pain raged in my body like a wild animal pent up in a steel cage. My throat felt worthless as a tool for eating, but I tried to be thankful that I could at least still breath. The sores and swelling choked my voice to a whisper. My head pounded relentlessly. The ringing in my right ear was incessant.

One rare evening at home, as my bone-pain peaked and the pulsating pain in my head hammered against my senses, I dragged my body up the stairs. The eight stairs might as well have been Mt. Everest. I screamed. My pain, frustration, and anger spewed out through tears and shrieks. I thrashed up each step, carpet fibers flying as my fingernails dug in like spikes in an iceberg. My mom offered to help, but in my determination, I refused.

My t-shirt stuck to my back as I finally flung myself into my bed, sweat seeping from every pore.

In a sigh of desperation, I begged God to let me die. The words began to flow, half-spoken through my cracked and strained vocal chords:

> "Lord, I really don't know what to say. I've never been one at a loss for words, but I am now. I don't know why You are doing this or what good could come from this, but I am slowly losing hope. This last scan wasn't good. In fact, it was awful. Even the doctors are wondering if this is even something we can continue to fight. I know this isn't news to You, but why? Why is this happening? I look over at Harley and wonder why You are going to take his mommy away from him. And, You know, Lord, I'm not scared to actually die. I'm really not. I can handle death because I know that when I close my eyes here on earth, I will open them in Heaven. However, the thought of leaving Harley is just too much to bear. Lord, I just don't know why You would bring this precious baby into our lives and then rip me out of his. I guess I'll never understand that. But, Your ways are not my ways. I love You Lord, I just can't figure it all out. I feel so bad for my family. David, I feel

so bad for him. I watch him look at me and cry. I know he has to be so overwhelmed, and I know he thinks I'm going to die. We all do. My dad and mom are pitiful. I watch them look at me. Sometimes they don't know I can see them staring at me and sobbing. They think I'm asleep. Lord, it is awful to watch people mourn me. So, here it is...If You aren't going to heal me like we are all praying for, then please, please, please just take me. I can't watch them mourn me. I can't bear to look at Harley's face light up when he looks at me because ALL I think about is how he is going to wonder where I went when I'm gone. How long will he think about me before he forgets? Lord, I can't take this. So, please, my prayer is that if it isn't Your will to heal me, then take me. The pain is bad today, Lord. Can You please help it ease just a little? I love You, Lord, and I do trust You. I may not ever understand, but I do love and trust You."

My relationship with God felt stagnant. With only one eye functioning, it was almost impossible to read my Bible. The words blurred together on the page, and the pain became too great after just a few words. I couldn't go to church. All I could do was pray, but I asked for relief and none came. I asked for healing and heaven seemed silent. I knew God was there. I knew He cared. I *knew* His promises were true, but it all *felt* hollow, like I just couldn't see what God wanted me to see.

My vice-grip on the steering wheel of my life had been pried lose. As I laid on my bed, I admitted my worthless attempt to manage my circumstances and relented. I admitted that the outcome of my cancer may be death, and I silently agreed. I didn't want to fight anymore.

My suffering was the least of my concerns. The anguish my suffering brought on my family seemed worse than death in that moment. My family didn't deserve this. Being the patient, I was also normally the comforter, but I couldn't even manage that through the pain and medication. Everyone strained to hold in their emotions around me, as mine sometimes spewed around like a rogue water hose. After weeks of intense emotional pressure, our seams were beginning to crack.

My dad, brother, and father-in-law had essentially become bachelors since our moms were always gone. Along with David and Krista, they tried to hold down jobs in the midst of such chaos and emotional turmoil. Lines of exhaustion filled my mom's face. She hadn't slept more than a few hours at a time in months. She knew I couldn't bear the suffering much longer. She begged David to hide his hunting rifles fearing I would get desperate enough to end my own pain.

After witnessing one of my worst days, my dad experienced severe chest pains. My mom was faced with a heart-wrenching decision: drive her husband to the hospital or stay with me and Harley. I was in no condition to care for a baby and no one else could get there in time.

Tearfully, my mom watched as my dad's truck pulled out of the driveway. As his taillights disappeared, she prayed that he would make it to the hospital in time if it was a heart attack.

Richard's doctor placed him on anxiety medication due to the pain and grief overwhelming his tender heart. Patsy, an emotional bedrock for many of us day in and day out, sobbed uncontrollably while driving home each night. My brother stayed busy organizing fund-raisers and taking care of things around my parents' house – desperate to push the worry and concern out of his mind through busyness. None of them deserved this.

I began preparing for the end. I wanted to take pictures constantly. My mom chuckled as I paraded my nurses through my hospital room, snapping photos with each one, like I was on the red carpet instead of on my deathbed. I took pictures with Harley and David daily. Despite my atrocious handwriting, I started a journal for Harley, chronicling my battle and recording things I wanted him to know. A few pieces of paper seemed like a feeble replacement for a mom, but I wanted to give him everything I could. I wanted him to hear my words, know how much I loved him, and know how hard I fought to stay with him.

David refused to talk about the looming possibility, but his doses of optimism were no longer able to comfort me as they had before. I would continue to pray and fight, but I had to be realistic. The test results told the story of a dying woman, and I wanted my family to be prepared.

One afternoon, I called my mom into my bedroom. As I started to discuss funeral arrangements, her hands covered her face and she shook her head.

"Mom, I need you to do this for me. I need to know that I helped prepare as much as I could." After laying out what I wanted for the funeral, I reached across the bed and handed her an envelope. It was addressed simply: To the New Mrs. Hallford.

My mom gasped.

"Mom, David's 25. He'll be a single dad. He will marry again. It's okay. I want him to. I just need you to make sure that she gets this." Tears streamed down my mom's face as she read silently.

To the New Mrs. Hallford,

I know this may seem strange, reaching out to you from beyond the grave, but I wanted to share a few things with you as you step into the shoes I used to fill. I know you won't do things the way I would have, and that's okay and to be expected. I just wanted to pass along some things I've learned about these two precious guys and to ask you for a few things.

First of all, thank you. Thank you for being willing to raise a little boy who isn't yours. I have only known him for a few months, but he is honestly the sweetest kid ever. (Hopefully he is past the acid reflux stage by now!) He loves to smile and loves to be held – probably too much. Sorry about that one. I've left you a journal that you can read to him or give him when he is old enough to read it for himself. I've left him letters to read on his milestone days – graduation and his wedding day. Please make sure he gets those.

Please continue to read to him each night and sing songs. "Jesus Loves Me" is always a favorite of ours. When David is at the fire station, please still take Harley to church. I know it is tough getting out the door on your own with a little one, but I want Harley to know that church is important even when Daddy has to work. My parents and friends are more than eager to help you out, if you need it.

Speaking of my parents, please remember to invite them to celebrations and let them see Harley regularly. I'm sure you have a family that loves Harley too, but my parents have lost so much already. I know they are scared they will lose their relationship with Harley and David. Please help make this a priority when you can. My parents are happy to help in any way, but I know once I'm gone, it may be awkward for them to push into situations.

I can't give you too much advice on parenting, since I've been a mom for about five minutes myself, but I can help you a little with

David. You will probably be married to him longer than I was, but I can give you a head start in some things I've learned. Don't let him handle the checkbook. Lord help us. If you don't know how to handle money, maybe take a class or hire an accountant. David is an amazing husband and father and an extremely capable firefighter and man of God...just don't give him the checkbook or the laundry basket.

I'm sure you already know he is a hunter. I think some people are born for certain things, and David was definitely born a hunter. So, all those dreams you have of family pumpkin patch days and hay rides in the fall, forget them. He will mess up any fall plans you have and he will eventually want to take Harley with him. Trust him with the guns and find a friend to go with you to the apple orchards and pumpkin patches. Learn what to do with venison, because you will have a lot of it. David's a bit like a caveman – he kills it, and expects you to be able to do something with it. Chili and spaghetti are my go to venison recipes, always served with a large glass of sweet tea.

Finally, please know that I am cheering you on. I'm not upset or angry that you are David's new wife. David and Harley need you and I am thankful that you are going to love them as I no longer can. Don't feel bad when they talk about me or if David cries at the memory of me. When David tosses his wedding ring in the air, it just means he's nervous or anxious. Rub his head and make him some coffee. He loves that. He loves you, and I'm thankful he does. The Lord has brought you to them, and y'all will be a new family. Harley will have the blessing of being loved by two moms. You will be the face my little boy remembers tucking him in every night. Give him a kiss from me when you do.

Cheering you on,
Ashley

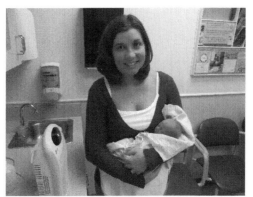
Harley's first doctor's appointment

Feeding Harley during his hospital stay, immediately following my cancer surgery.

Harley's Baby Dedication Service

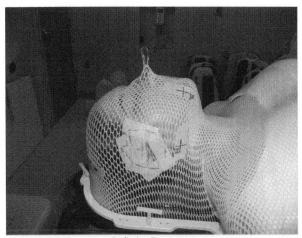

Radiation Treatment

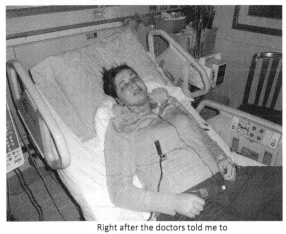

Right after the doctors told me to
start taking pictures for Harley

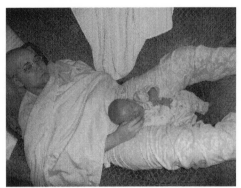
Resting with Harley during my sickest time

Visit from my sweet baby

Valentine's Day 2008

Selfie plea to David and my mom, "Come get me."

May 2008, as my eye began to open

Krista's visits were always a lifeline

Easter 2018

David's parents - Richard and Patsy

My parents – Sheila and Tommy

Dr. Miller and I on the set of Megyn Kelly Today

David, Krista, Stephanie and I in New York City May 2018

Chapter 17
The Clipboard

"The effectual fervent prayer of a righteous man availeth much." James 5:16b

I have always handled the money. It started when David showed me his checkbook once while we were dating. Along the bottom line of the register in flat blank ink, he simply wrote, "What the bank says I have." A laugh had burst out of my mouth like biscuits from a Pillsbury can. I have a type-A personality combined with a finance degree, and I couldn't fathom a world where I would simply write down the balance that the bank said I had, trusting their calculations over mine. With little prodding, David was more than happy to hand over any and all finance duties to me that day.

Our modest earnings early in our marriage forced us to stay on a budget, or at least try. We paid our bills on time, contributed to our church and by looking for bargains and deals, we occasionally had enough left over for vacations or home improvements. Sometimes, however, when you look for bargains, you get exactly what you pay for, like the time we wanted to replace our floors. Lulu had ruined our carpet after just a few months of lazy pet parenting. We called a discount floor company from a TV ad. They promised to complete the job in just one day.

As the clock rolled past 1:00 AM, we realized in our exhaustion that cheaper is not always better.

Unfortunately, there is not a lot of bargain hunting or deal shopping during cancer treatments. You don't compare imaging facilities to see which one offers the lowest price. There's not a lot of margin for negotiating radiation and chemotherapy costs when you are in a fight for your life. Supply and demand wins that battle every time. So, during the midst of the emotional and physical roller coaster of battling cancer, the bills started rolling in like a tsunami.

In typical fashion, I did not let cancer stand in my way of important things that only I could do – like paying bills. I'm sure David rolled his eyes as he complied with my insistence on paying the bills, just as my mom had lovingly done with the checks for our church members. Ignoring the fact that I could only see out of one eye, that the pounding in my head made words seem to vibrate across the page, that the bone pain made lifting a pencil feel like lifting a barbell, and that I had pain medicine clouding my mind, I continued to grasp tasks within my control. I would sit in the hospital bed, scribbling checks, recording payments, and filing bills.

In anticipation of becoming a family of three, we had purchased a new Honda CR-V the weekend before we learned I had cancer. Free advice – don't buy a new car if you have a huge knot in your neck that may be cancer. Talk about bad timing. On top of the mounting medical bills, new car payment, and our mortgage, we had a baby. Due to his acid reflux, Harley's doctor wanted him on the pre-mixed liquid formula, which also happened to be the most expensive. The emotional strain mounted as I watched the bills pile up. I cried every time I opened an envelope and told David we needed to research how to file bankruptcy.

God has the ability to beautifully orchestrate situations in which we must depend on Him. While I still struggled to juggle the balls of my life from a hospital bed, I could not write enough checks to cover the bills. The money ran out before I could even make a dent. The radiation bill alone was $89,000 – more than David would make in the next *two years*.

We were forced to put all of our everyday expenses on credit cards as we used David's paycheck to keep a roof over our heads and begin to make payments on the medical bills. I was in the perfect position to finally have to look to the Lord for provision. I couldn't work it out or make the money stretch. I couldn't get a part-time job or bargain hunt my way out of this one. All I could do was wait.

I'm sure God could have generated a computer error, wiping our balance clean with the hospital, labs, and doctors, however He chose to work as He often does – through His people. Checks, cash, and gift cards began arriving in the mail, gift cards for everywhere from Kroger to Macys and Gymboree. Through Carepage updates, our church family and friends kept up to date with any needs we had. Bags of groceries, diapers, formula, and wipes would show up on our door step. Casseroles and crockpots, filled to the brim with southern comfort, lined our counters and the shelves of our fridge. The sacrifice and generosity of friends, family, and total strangers overwhelmed us.

My brother worked tirelessly with local organizations and business to organize fundraisers. He helped organize a movie night at a local theater, coordinated a motorcycle ride, and set up an account for donations. My OB/GYN office organized a Tennis Tournament to raise money to cover our medical expenses. As word spread of our need, families organized yard sales, sold t-shirts, made bracelets, and washed cars.

One of the largest fundraising avenues was through donut sales. I love donuts almost as much as Frappuccinos. Nothing is better than a warm donut, right out of the oven, with the sugar that has just started to crust around the billowy-soft dough, oozing out the side of your mouth. I guess this love for donuts runs deep in the south. Frequent donut sales rivaled my previous job salary, with one sale raising just over $5,000. That's a lot of Krispy Kremes!

We saw God providing for us exactly how His Word promised – giving to us our daily bread. While, no one paid off the massive radiation bill with one check, we could clearly see God's faithfulness in thousands of small ways.

David: *As a husband and a father, I wanted nothing more than to provide for my family. I knew I didn't have a fancy job, but I worked hard to carve out our little piece of the*

American dream doing something that I loved. I went to work every day to help people and save lives. As a man, I wanted to save my wife and take her pain but was helpless to do anything. Then I was hit with a wall of debt that I couldn't begin to pay. Honestly though, I didn't even think about the money. I would have gladly emptied what little money we had in the bank, if it meant saving my family.

As February came to a close, Dr. Miller continued to consult with the oncologist team in Boston to develop a new chemo regimen. Given the scans, we all knew it was a last-ditch effort to combat the rapidly-spreading cancer. I was scheduled to start the new chemo medicine on March 8th.

David*: Growing up in a small Baptist church, I experienced what it meant for people at church to feel like family. However, this felt different. It was as if people of our church formed a wall around us, covering us in prayer. The roots of my faith grew deeper as my humility increased. I saw the Lord meet tangible needs every day. Every realization of His provision inched my faith toward a greater understanding of His love for me and my family.*

Then one night, I found myself on the floor of my living room, crying out to God, begging him to end Ashley's suffering. For a moment, it was as if literal arms reached around my shoulders, hugging me tightly. I have never felt the presence of God like I did in that moment. I cried as I rested in my Father's arms, feeling His love overflowing in my heart. Then it was as if He whispered in my ear, "She's going to be okay." Relief washed over me. I had never doubted God. I trusted Him, but I knew He may decide to take Ashley home. After that moment, I just watched in anticipation at what the Lord was going to do.

I didn't have to wait long.

A lady in our church had a massive stroke around the same time Ashley was diagnosed. Right before Ashley started the new chemo medication, a few ladies in our church approached our pastor, asking him to organize a month-long, 24-hour prayer and fast vigil. Our church prayed, and we knew what fasting was I guess, but we had never done anything like this.

The next Sunday, our pastor passed around a clipboard, with a slot for each day of the month. When someone signed up for a slot, they were committing to pray and fast for 24 hours. The slots on the clipboard were full before it made it around the room. I cried as Brother Eddie called and told me what people were willing to do for us. Their faith strengthened my own.

On February 23, with the start of the new chemo treatments just a few weeks away, Ashley had to be admitted to the hospital again. Her white blood cell count and coherence to daily activities was at a new low, while her pain and frustration with another hospital stay was at a new high. One night, while sitting at the fire station, I picked up my phone after a series of beeps. Ashley had snapped a selfie of her alone in her hospital room, sending it to both Sheila and me with the caption, "Could someone *please just come get me?" I choked back tears, but then I froze.*

As I stared at the grainy picture, my heart leaped. Ashley's eyelid that had been closed for weeks seemed to be slightly cracked. I assumed it couldn't be possible and didn't want to get Ashley's hopes up in case it was just the poor picture quality or the angle of the camera, but I thought about that clipboard full of names of people from our church. The prayer schedule had just started. Could this be God answering prayers already?

A few days after being discharged from the hospital, I experienced a series of flashes in my good eye. My heart sank as I pictured the brain tumor swelling and pushing toward my other optic nerve. I went to see Dr. Spector that afternoon, fearing the worst. In what felt like a rare moment of good news, he reported that everything looked normal. While he could not explain what caused the flashes, he did not see any cause for concern with that eye. He also noticed the movement of my right eye lid.

"How long have you been able to open your eye?" he asked with a hint of optimism in his voice.

While in the hospital, the pain medication clouded my lucidity enough at first that I couldn't be sure my eye had actually started to open, but over the past few days the progress had been impossible to ignore.

"It just started about two days ago. It opened just a crack at first and now when I'm not exhausted, it actually opens about half-way," I reported.

He noted the next MRI date, scheduled for the end of the March.

"Let's see what things look like then," he replied, the door clicking behind him as he left the room.

March 8, 2008

Through the slit in my eye, I could see the tech in the corner of the room, mixing the chemo medication. I prayed.

"God that man is mixing up what seems to be my last hope to stay on this earth, yet I know that You are really the only hope I have. You're the only hope I've ever had. I admit I have blazed my own trail at times during this process, leaving a mess in my wake. Fully trusting You has been harder than I imagined that it would be. Having never experienced anything life-altering before, I thought I had it. I thought I could handle my life and that I only needed to bother You for the big things. I hope that things are different in the future, if I even have one, but for today I have just one request: let this work or just take me home. I can't plan or control my way out of this. All I can do is lie here in this chair, watching the medicine drip into my body. I know people at church are praying and fasting, seriously asking You to intervene. I can't believe people would do that for me. I can't believe that You would love me the way You do either. So, here I am. My body is completely broken, and I have nothing to offer. I ask for exactly what I do not deserve – Your mercy in healing me here or relieving my family of their suffering and giving me ultimate healing in heaven."

A peace unlike anything I had ever experienced washed over me, as I drifted off to sleep while the first few drops trickled through the tube.

March 24, 2008

I stared at the white capsule surrounding me and wondered if this would be my last MRI. I knew if the results were bad that I wouldn't have much longer to live. Given my diagnosis in January, my doctors were surprised I had lived this long. I seemed to be on borrowed time. I had made up my mind that if the results showed that the cancer had spread further, then I would stop treatments and just enjoy the time I had left with Harley, David, and my family. I wanted to at least have a few days or weeks with them free of the sickness and pain that the chemotherapy and treatments brought.

David and I made the short drive from the MRI facility to Dr. Spector's office, weaving through the traffic and narrow streets of Atlanta. We waited breathlessly for him to appear, our moods mirroring our outlooks – David expected the best, while I anticipated the worst. David's red shirt wrinkled against my wrist, as his hand gripped mine. The door squeaked open.

Dr. Spector's glasses sat on the end of his nose, his white coat hanging neatly over his blue shirt and tie. His brown shoes clicked across the floor as he sat down, rolled his chair over to the wall, and flicked on a switch, illuminating the MRI scans. His voice, coated with cautious optimism pointed to the scans taken just a few hours earlier. The pain medication that clouded my brain made the medical jargon sound like someone speaking a foreign language. I glanced at David, his eyes fixed on the doctor, wondering if he could comprehend the words that were sailing past me. Dr. Spector then turned back toward the scans, tracing the outline of my brain with the back of his pen.

"Ashley, your brain is symmetrical again along these lines. And see this vein? It was completely hidden by the tumor on your last scans."

I blinked repeatedly, my mouth slightly open, as I stared at his face like an American tourist trying to decipher Spanish in the middle of Mexico City. I muddled the words together in my brain and managed to push them out of my mouth.

"Dr. Spector, what are you saying?"

His eyes widened and a smile broke out across his soft, wrinkled face.

"Ashley, your brain tumor is gone."

Chapter 18
Light in the Tunnel

"Casting all your care upon Him;
for He careth for you." I Peter 5:7

I sat motionless, transfixed by the scans in front of me. I had built up dreadful anticipation that the scans would show that the tumor now stretched further across my brain. Words echoed around me until David finally tugged my arm, coaxing me back to reality.

"So, what does this mean?" I asked, a smile widening across my face.

"It means we can be cautiously optimistic that the radiation treatments have worked. There is still this area here," he said, pointing to a patch of white on the scans, "but it just appears to be scar tissue."

We climbed in our CR-V. As I clicked my seatbelt, I noticed tears rolling down David's cheeks. He slid his hand across the seat, wrapping his fingers around mine. His grip tightened as his words poured out.

David: *"Father, thank You. Thank You. We don't know what You have for us on this journey, but thank You for this news today. You are good and we trust You." I leaned over and kissed my wife, stunned at the news we had received. While her body was still racked with pain and disease, this news brought a wind of hope in my sails. Dr. Spector had told us months before that the tumor was somewhere only God's hands could go, and we had just witnessed a work that could have only been His.*

Driving home, I waffled between elation and dread. While this was certainly amazing news that I wanted to shout from the rooftops, I felt I had to be cautious to keep it in perspective. After all, the tumor in my neck was gone too. Cancer is often a dance of one step forward, three steps back. I still had innumerable tumors on my lungs which would suffocate me if something didn't change.

The next day, as Harley and I settled into our spot in the living room with his Harley Davidson onesie fit snuggly around him, I thought about Janet, the woman that lit up the room with her smile during our radiation treatments. I had received word from her sister that morning that Janet had lost her battle with cancer. Her death rocked my fragile faith. My faith and optimism paled in comparison to hers, and yet she died. Even with the positive MRI, I knew that the same end could be awaiting me. I cried as I wondered about the questions we all seem to grapple with at some point in our lives – why does God heal some people and not others? Why did I deserve positive news and she had to die a slow and painful death?

I pushed aside those thoughts. God was God, and I had to trust that. I had to trust my story to Him, just like

Janet trusted Him with hers. I knew she would have celebrated the news of my brain tumor with me if she could, her manicured hands clapping and raising in praise to Jesus. Instead of dwelling on my sadness, I know she would have wanted me to celebrate the mercy God had shown to me and appreciate every day I had to live with my family. I thought of her warm smile as I looked down at Harley, smiling in his sleep. I smiled too.

***

The next few weeks were a blur of chemo treatments, shots and pain medication – the same rhythm that had dictated my life for months. Fatigue plagued me as my body struggled under the weight of cancer and treatments. The bone pain from the Neulasta shots seemed to increase every time. Mercifully, the throbbing in my head eased slightly since the tumor in my brain was no longer pressing against my nerves.

Another round of MRI and CT scans was planned for April 15 to monitor the tumors on my lungs and liver. If the brain tumor had responded positively to treatments, I was cautiously optimistic that maybe the other tumors had as well. Our church had just concluded the month-long prayer and fasting schedule that they had implemented the first week of March. God had clearly worked during that time. The other young lady they had been praying for, who had the massive stroke, made amazing strides during those weeks as well, defying all medical possibilities for her recovery. The bad news had outweighed the good so many times though, that I tempered my optimism with a strong dose of my characteristic realism.

The day of the scans came, and we anxiously awaited the results, sitting in Dr. Miller's office. David leaned against the wall, tapping his boot on the ground with nervous energy. My mom sat in the chair next to him, her folded hands resting against her black pants. When Dr. Miller walked in, her mood seemed lighter than ever before, like a weight had been lifted from her slender shoulders.

"Ashley, your scans look good…"

My mom let out a sigh so forcefully that I wondered if she had been holding her breath the whole time we had been in the room. Tears welled up in her eyes.

Dr. Miller continued, "All of the tumors on your lungs are smaller than on the previous scans and some of the tumors are completely gone. The tumors are clearly responding to the treatments. We are not out of the woods yet, but this is definitely a step in the right direction."

In that moment, another breath of fresh, hopeful air had been pumped in our lungs. Just as with the brain tumor results, I wanted to jump up and down, but hesitated to celebrate fully, fearing a premature celebration would end in devastation if the tides shifted.

I looked into the faces of three people that felt just as relieved as I did, and I was reminded that cancer is not a solo journey. Family, friends, doctors, nurses, and medical staff all walk the journey alongside the patient. Their commitment and emotional skin in the game may vary, but they all feel the weight of this crushing, unpredictable disease. The tears and heartache, joy and laughter were centered on me. I felt thankful for having such caring and loving people to support me on this journey.

As I rested at home that afternoon, tired from traveling to the doctor's office and emotionally worn out from the anticipation and subsequent results, my mom's phone was a flurry of activity. She called and texted half the county, telling everyone the positive results of the scans. I eventually retreated to the bedroom to escape the wave of noise that came with each phone call.

Fear fell upon me once again a few days later when my jaw began to swell around the site of my initial tumor. Dreading the worst, I dashed to my phone to make an appointment, determined to go in that day, whether they had an appointment available or not. The doctor immediately ordered an MRI just to be cautious. All of the good news I had received could not counteract the weight of concern I felt during that scan. I knew if the scale started to tip back in the other direction, there would be few options since the doctors had exhausted virtually all treatment possibilities.

Dr. Miller reviewed the scan report. An area did light up on the scan, which is generally not a good sign. However, the radiologist noted that the questionable area appeared to be scar tissue from the tumor removal surgery.

A negative bone scan two weeks later would temporarily put to rest any fears that the cancer had metastasized to my bones. Temporarily, because for a cancer patient, the fear is never gone. Even after the scans are clear, the fear of recurrence always remains.

May, June, and July followed a predictable pattern. Every three weeks I would receive chemotherapy, a Neulasta shot the following day, and would feel crummy for the next ten to fourteen days. The predictability of my symptoms during this time brought some relief to me, David, and our families. We knew which days would be the worst and generally when I would start to feel better. The one week in the middle felt a little like normal life, a shadow of what our old life had been, but certainly calmer than the roller coaster we had experienced for the past four months. Our moms were needed less during that week and could begin to pick up the pieces of the lives that they had dropped in November. David returned to work on a more normal schedule. Krista continued to call nightly to check in and see how things were going and say good night to Harley.

On good days, my mom and I would go shopping or go out to lunch, with Harley as our constant companion. On his days off, David and I would grocery shop, go see a movie, or just hang out at home. We relished the mundane, everyday activities we had once taken for granted. One thoughtful gift card sent me down a habitual pattern of pedicures as soon as the effects of each chemo treatment began to wear off. My doctor warned me against pedicures or manicures because of the risk of infection. While I understood the risk of infection was extremely high due to my compromised immune system, sometimes the nail salon calls to a southern girl and she just cannot say no. I took every precaution I could – I basically paid for someone else to just paint my toes. Much to the confusion of the nail technicians, I passed on the pre-painting foot bath and opted for just a calf message and coat of paint. Few things can make a girl feel pretty like freshly polished toes. With no hair or eyebrows, I felt like I needed all the help I could get. My doctor eventually won that battle however, when I came down with a nasty case of cellulitis on the back of my legs. I quickly agreed that I would just have to settle for painting my toes at home.

Surprisingly, a girl can still have a bad hair day, even when she doesn't have any hair. Our health insurance paid for a wig, but I did not wear it often. I even bought another one, for a little variety, but didn't like that one any better. They felt exactly like wearing an itchy sock on your head, which during the heat of Georgia summers, felt miserable. So, I wore scarves most of the time, other than to church. Around the house though, I enjoyed going au natural.

Hospital stays decreased, but were still necessary at times. They would normally come the week after chemo, when even the continued high doses of medicated patches failed to control the pain enough for me to remain at home. I would suffer at home, not wanting to be admitted again, until finally David or my mom would insist on taking me to the ER. The round robin game of taking care of me and Harley reappeared during those hospital stints, with David, Patsy, and my mom taking turns at home and at the hospital.

At the end of the month, MRI and CT scans were scheduled to monitor the tumors. The scans felt so routine, I could flow from one step to the next with little instruction. After the MRI, I sat up, ready to receive the shot of contrast dye in preparation for the CT scan immediately following. The nurse injected the shot into my upper arm, her dark blue scrubs brushing against my leg as she turned to dispose of the needle. Minutes later, she grabbed my arm, stretching it out over my legs.

A rash spread over the underside of my arm like wall to wall carpet.

"What is that?" I asked, shocked at my own level of concern. After having a body riddled with cancer, you would think a rash wouldn't phase me.

"It looks like you are having an allergic reaction to the dye. We will have to cancel the CT scan for today."

She scurried out the door and returned a few moments later, a small plastic cup in her right hand. She dumped four pills in my outstretched hand and gave me the plastic cup, full of what I could only assume was hospital tap water. I swallowed the fist-full of pills.

"But how could that happen? I've had this scan multiple times before?"

"It just happens sometimes. Given all your body has endured, you may have these types of problems more frequently."

Perfect, I thought. Add it to the list.

I returned the following week for another CT scan, this time without the contrast dye and accompanying allergic reaction. Dr. Miller reviewed the results with us that afternoon in her office.

"The number of the tumors in your lungs continues to decrease and the scan of your brain continues to look clear." Her smile radiated across the room as she turned to leave, her blonde hair falling over her shoulder as her black high heels clicked against the tile floor. Walking to the car, I felt like I was riding a wave of good news, unsure if it would crash around me at any moment. Despite my relentless fears, I thanked God for the good news and determined to continue to enjoy each day He gave me to live.

***

July 28, 2008

The July sun baked my pale skin as we lumbered across the parking lot, feeling like our shoes might sink into the melting asphalt before we could make it to the glass doors just beyond the sidewalk. Harley's feet bounced in the car seat to the rhythm of David's stride. The diaper bag hung on my mom's shoulder as she followed us in, thankful for the blast of cool air that welcomed us in from the heat. I billowed my maxi dress, sweat already dripping down my back from the short walk.

We filed over to a couch against the back wall of the waiting room. Harley's eyelids were heavy as he scanned his new surroundings. David leaned his head back, his eyelid's as heavy as Harley's. With our moms not staying through the night as often, David and I were full-time parents again. Harley still woke up during the night, sometimes for long stretches, hence the heavy eyelids all around.

My mom patted my knee as she cooed at Harley, oblivious to the fact he needed to go to sleep. She was in the grandma zone. I looked at her eyes as she smiled at him. The lines in her face seemed to have deepened a bit over the past nine months, almost as if the sorrow and sleepless nights had been sewn into her. Watching her child battle cancer had been horrific and painful, while the joy of being with Harley made the days bittersweet. The last few doctor's reports had seemed to ease her sorrow and bring back the smile I had always known from my mom. The kind-hearted teasing and jesting had begun to creep back into conversations as the load of her heart seemed to grow a little lighter.

Yet, the weight still loomed over us. We sat waiting to talk to my oncologist. Our moods still breathed an air of soberness as we walked down the hallway, turning the corner into the brightly lit exam room. The pale blue walls faded gently into the cream tiles along the floor. I balanced myself on the edge of the exam table, my mom and David sitting in the chairs next to me.

Dr. Miller peeked in, her usual smile greeting us as she slipped through the doorway. Her baby pink shirt visible just above her lab coat complimented her matching patent leather pumps and beige skirt. I appreciated her smart fashion almost as much as her medical skills. She chatted briefly about Harley and asked how things were at home. Through her pleasantries, I sensed a new tension in her voice. I couldn't place it. Then she gently rolled her chair toward me, planting one foot next to the base of the exam table, the other crossed neatly over her knee.

"Ashley, I'm just going to read you exactly what the radiologist reported."

My heart seemed to stop beating in my chest. The room froze around me and she seemed to been speaking in slow motion. I glanced at David and my mom. They seemed to be frozen too. It was clear. Dr. Miller had news to share, news seemingly too massive to form the words for herself. As the stopwatch on the moment of time seemed to release, I gripped the side of the table, bracing for what I assured myself would be a massive blow.

Chapter 19
Cancer Free

"Many are the afflictions of the righteous; but the Lord delivereth him out of them all." Ps. 34:19

"It says, 'No evidence of disease present'."

Her words hung in midair until my brain could process what they actually meant. Looking up from the chart, her eyes met mine.

"So, what does that mean?" I stuttered. The words were simple and the message was impossible to miss, yet my brain struggled to comprehend the weight they carried.

"I never thought I would say these words to you, Ashley, but it means you are in remission. You are cancer free." Dr. Miller flashed her signature smile, tears brimming in the corners of her eyes.

Despite her clear explanation, I continued to blink in confusion. Finally, I managed to break my gaze from Dr. Miller and turned toward David and my mom. In unison we erupted into tears of joy and celebration. We all hugged, free from the terminal weight that had burdened us for the past seven months.

I smiled down at Harley, groggily looking around having been startled awake by our raucous celebration and thanked God for letting me be his mom a little while longer. I realized this whole saga – my struggle for survival – would only be known to him through stories and pictures. He wouldn't have to live with the daily pain of never knowing his mom. I didn't even know how to thank God for what He had done.

David: *Tears splashed down my cheeks as I took in the news, my emotions unapologetic. We had not expected any significant news that day; it was a routine follow up after scans. Just five months earlier, Ashley had been given little hope to live more than a few weeks, yet now remission? It was unbelievable, nothing short of miraculous. God had healed her. I knew He could, and I reveled in the joy He had given us. I felt unworthy of all the blessings surrounding me. Ashley was cancer free. Our healthy son sat next to my feet. Dr. Miller, whom God had providentially placed in our path to provide wisdom in this journey, shared our excitement, and Sheila represented our family and friends who had sacrificed so much over the past few months. While I knew I didn't have any special reason to deserve these blessings, I thanked God for each one of them.*

I walked toward Ashley, her beauty radiating from within. The cancer had ravaged her body and taken her hair, yet she was the most beautiful person I had ever seen. She had fought through unimaginable physical and emotional pain. As I wrapped her in my arms, I knew she could have given up, easily could have said the pain was too much, yet she fought for us. She fought to stay with us and against all odds, and by God's grace, she had won.

Sheila: *I hadn't even planned on going to the doctor with them that day. We had no idea of the news we would hear. It was a moment I will never forget. The tunnel we were walking through had been so very dark, and I didn't know if we would ever hear the word "remission." I just sat there, weeping like a baby, thanking God for His faithfulness. Not only had He healed Ashley, He kept His promise to never leave us. He truly carried us every step of the way.*

Dr. Miller echoed our deepest thoughts, "God was 100 percent in this. He may have used me as a tool, but this work was His."

Gathering my thoughts and emotions, I wondered what would happen next. I didn't think I would live past my cancer diagnosis. Suddenly, a future without cancer stood in front of me, but I couldn't shape what days would look like without pain, treatments, and constant medication.

"So, am I finished with treatments? Is that it? I'm cured?"

"Well, you have certainly earned a few weeks off of chemotherapy. Take some time off and enjoy it with your family. Remember what it is like to feel normal! After about six weeks however, I would recommend a maintenance round of chemo lasting about six months.

229

We can reduce the dosage to help ease the side effects. This is an important step. While there may not be any signs of cancer on the scans, this round of chemo will help fight off any floater cancer cells that may still be present. If allowed to linger, floater cells could lodge and create another mass anywhere in the body."

I agreed to the next round of chemo, wanting to do everything to ensure that the cancer didn't return.

"What are the chances that this could come back?" I asked, not really sure I wanted to know the answer.

"There is a 75-90 percent chance of recurrence," she reluctantly replied.

Her response sucked some of the celebratory spirit from the room. After the surgery to remove the initial tumor, I thought I had won the battle over cancer. This time I would not be so naïve. Secretly, I felt the cancer would come back one day, but I resolved to enjoy every moment I had until then. I hugged Dr. Miller's petite frame as we turned to leave. The "thank you" I offered seemed feeble for someone who had just saved my life.

***

The next six weeks were a sweet season of celebration and renewal for our family. As the news of my remission spread, we were inundated with celebratory calls, texts, hugs, and visits.

Brother Eddie: *I remember standing in the pulpit reading the doctor's report to our congregation. Shouts of praise erupted with the words "no evidence of disease present." I have never witnessed another event bond a church together like Ashley's cancer did for our church. Her story became a stake in the ground – a clear picture of God's healing power and His faithfulness. Everyone emerged from the cocoon of the trial with a new perspective – our church, their family, and especially Ashley and David. I saw their faith deepen and their relationship with each other blossom. God truly turned the ashes of a hopeless situation into beauty.*

We planned a trip to the beach with our families to celebrate. We spent the week relaxing while gushing over Harley, now nine months old. His cheerful claps and splashes kept our cameras busy.

Our pastor, knowing our fourth anniversary would fall during our trip, arranged for a limo service to pick us up for a fancy dinner. With Harley in multiple safe hands, we got ready for our first date night since having Harley. With an itchy wig in place and eyebrows painted on by my mom for the occasion, we enjoyed a quiet dinner out and reflected on the events of the past year. We could not have imagined a year earlier what was in store. As we prayed together that night, I silently wondered what would be lurking in the year to come. I prayed we would have the most boring year of our lives!

In late September, I began the six-month round of maintenance chemo. It felt strange sitting in a room full of patients knowing I was in remission. I felt almost guilty.

However, with a port in my chest, regular chemotherapy treatments, patches on my back, a daily pill regimen, and no hair, remission didn't seem quite as glamorous as I had imagined. I longed for the day when all the wires would truly be cut.

Dr. Miller continued to monitor my progress with scans every three months to ensure that there were no signs of recurrence. Every scan brought high anxiety with equally high relief when I received a clear report.

As Harley's first birthday approached, I threw myself into planning a gargantuan celebration during every spare minute between the days of feeling crummy from chemo. Having missed out on virtually all of his milestones over the past year, I wanted his first birthday to be a celebration to remember.

On the big day, a puppy-dog theme erupted in the party location at a beautiful neighborhood clubhouse rented by a family friend. Our house would have been too small to accommodate the crowd expected at the celebration. Close to sixty family members and friends packed the room, all showering Harley with presents and well wishes. Dressed in red overalls, he greeted everyone around the room with smiles. He thoroughly enjoyed diving into his birthday cake before collapsing in exhaustion on the short drive home.

One could argue that between his birthday party in mid-November to Christmas just a few weeks later, I went a little overboard with gifts and celebration. However, having survived one round of cancer and living with the possibility of another looming on the horizon, festivities seemed fitting.

February 25, 2009

The time had finally come for my last treatment. I settled into the chair as the nurse pulled back my shirt, revealing my port. I remembered the first chemo treatment – the fear and uncertainty that surrounded me that day. The infusion room no longer seemed scary. I looked forward to visiting with nurses that felt more like family. While I loathed the side effects on my body, I knew that God has used chemotherapy to save my life from stage-four, seemingly terminal cancer. I welcomed the last treatment with elation.

Knowing the sorrow facing the patients in the large infusion room and not wanting to appear to be callous to their plight in our celebration, I opted for the smaller, private infusion room for my last treatment. We arranged snacks, drinks and a cake along the counter. During my treatment, nurses and staff members stopped by for a few bites and congratulated me on my remission and end of treatment.

The frosting on the cake billowed in my mouth, reminding me of all the frappuccinos the year before. I reflected on where I had been and what the Lord had brought me through. I had now been cancer free for almost seven months. I prayed that the odds stacked against me would not turn out to be true. I once again savored the joy, knowing that my story could have turned

233

out differently. God didn't have to reach down and heal me physically, but I knew His work had been much deeper than just my tumors.

While the tumors were innumerable to men, He could count every one. He knew every shape and size, but He also knew the condition of my heart. Far more than a healed body, He wanted me to see Him. He wanted me to see past myself and my list and schedules. He wanted me to know that He was in control all along. Sitting in that room, I realized He had been at the helm the whole time, even when I clawed and fought for control I never had. His mercy and goodness washed over me in a new way, and I was humbled by His unending grace, forgiveness, and healing. I didn't know if I would ever have to walk through cancer again, but I knew if I did, things would be different the next time around. I would have a bedrock of trust to anchor me in the midst of the storm. I knew He would guide me and protect me. Maybe I would die of cancer one day, but I had a new-found peace that He was in control.

Chapter 20
Detox

---

*"For He knoweth our frame; He remembereth that
we are dust."* Ps. 103: 14

In late April, I once again sat in Dr. Miller's office, awaiting scan results. My eye had returned to full function and my hair had just started to grow beneath my scarf. Having been off chemo for two months, I felt like a new person. My energy increased gradually as the weeks passed. While I was thankful for any positive progress, I wished my energy would increase exponentially to keep up with Harley's unlimited supply.

"Your scans look great, Ashley."

Knowing the chances of recurrence, every clear scan brought welcomed relief.

Just one obstacle now stood in the way of me feeling like I could put my cancer journey in my rear-view mirror. Through the remission news and maintenance chemo, I had continued my routine of patches and pain medication. While my steroid regimen had been weaned after radiation therapy, no one had mentioned the pain medications and I had never thought to ask before then.

The patches on my back had to be rotated to different positions with each application because they could cause skin damage. After fifteen months of constant application, available space was quickly running out. Raw, irritated patches lined my back. Every time I applied a new patch I wondered why – why did I still need these if I was in remission and my treatments were complete?

"When am I able to come off this pain medication?" I asked Dr. Miller, assuming the response would be simple.

"It is definitely time to start that process," she said. "I will refer you to a pain management doctor who specializes in this area. He can work with you to develop a plan to come off the medication."

I left confused at what she meant by "process." Uneducated on the complexities of pain medications and the effects they can have on the body, I had just assumed that one day I would stop taking the medication and simply take the patches off my back. I did not realize that after being on high doses for eighteen months, my body had grown dependent on the drugs. My brain had literally rewired itself, allowing the pain medications to fire in places my brain had once fired before. Ripping the medication away would be jarring to my body and brain.

I saw glimpses of this process before I ever realized what was happening. With my pain virtually gone, except for sporadic headaches, I would occasionally forget to reapply a new patch after a shower. Within a few hours, I would experience intense pain, battle chills, feel restless, and become irritable. While I noticed the symptoms would subside after I applied a new patch, I didn't recognize the connection to a deep dependence my body had developed.

Consequently, I was not mentally prepared for the consultation with the pain management doctor the following week. He laid out his plan to wean me off the medication.

"First, we will decrease your dosage through the patches by cutting them little-by-little with each application. Next, we will gradually decrease your dosage of Dilaudid. Finally, I will prescribe Methadone once you are ready to transition off the pain medicine completely. It will bridge the gap and ease you through any withdrawal symptoms." He pushed his thick black glasses up his nose as he concluded, "The whole process should take about a year."

A laugh burst across the room before I could stop it.

"A year?" I retorted, thinking I must have misunderstood him. His silence assured me I had not been mistaken. His stone-faced response deepened my concern.

"No, actually I am interested in just stopping the medication. Like, now. I don't want to take medicine that I don't need for another year."

His measured response morphed into frustration as he spewed out the possible consequences of what he considered a reckless decision. "You could die if you attempted to stop the medications completely. In the very least, you could experience hallucinations, severe pain, and even suicidal thoughts or actions. Your body would not be able to sustain such careless action."

He could sense my resolve, despite his passionate rebuttal. We eventually compromised on a new plan that would make changes immediately yet still provide a gradual reduction over a shorter period of time. He agreed to stopping all oral pain medication and advised me to begin cutting my patches down by one quarter of their original size. In place of the pain medication, I would begin taking Methadone. I reluctantly agreed to the new plan.

At home later that night, I marched around the house with a paper bag, collecting every bottle of prescription medication I could find. I walked to my bathroom, dumping each one into the toilet. (I realize now there are much safer ways to dispose of narcotics!) My mom curiously followed me upstairs, unsure of what my purposeful march had been about. She watched as each pill splashed into the bowl, my satisfaction and fury evident. As I shoved the knob down and the last pill sloshed down the drain, my mom joked, "A lot of drug addicts would be jealous right now."

"Well, I am certainly not going to be one of them," I snapped.

I obediently took the Methadone as prescribed and began trimming down my pain patches, however my frustration grew as I thought about my situation. Methadone is designed to block the "high" one receives from opioids, easing withdrawal symptoms. It is therefore, commonly used to help drug addicts get clean. However,

I had taken drugs for cancer — I wasn't a drug addict. I hadn't abused the medication I had been prescribed, and yet my treatment plan mirrored that of a drug addict. After just one dose, I knew something was terribly wrong.

David: *Ashley was not herself when the cancer was at its worst. Steroids, radiation, chemo, and pain medication left her in a fog while the pain riddled her body. However, since she had been in remission, she had started coming out of the medication fog. I felt like I had my wife back.*

The detox process hit me like an unexpected blow to an already bruised back. Like Ashley, I just assumed she would stop the medicine when she didn't need it anymore. I figured if she could survive stage-four cancer, detox would be easy. Boy, was I wrong!

Immediately after the first dose of Methadone, I could see her body begin to slow and her responses became sluggish. She couldn't put coherent sentences together. I clasped her face in my hands, but her eyes seemed to look right past me. As a firefighter, I had seen people high on drugs — Ashley looked exactly like that. I hoped her body would adjust to the medicine and she would snap out of the haze that had surrounded her.

Over the next few days, she would fade in and out of lucidity. We couldn't leave her alone. Sheila and my mom continued to rotate in and out to help with Harley and to help keep an eye on Ashley while I worked. Then, she started saying things a husband should never hear his wife say. The woman I knew and loved fell completely behind a cloud of what I could only assume was drug induced behavior.

"This is just too hard. I can't do this. I just want to die, David. I can't do this." While I knew Ashley would never want to hurt herself, I couldn't be sure what influence the drugs would have on her. Tears slid down my face as I locked my guns in the cabinet, hiding the key in my truck. I cried out to God.

"Lord, haven't we been through enough? I don't know what to do. She's doing what the doctors told her to do, but I am scared. Please protect my wife. Please don't take her from me now, not after all we've been through. I know You can fix this. Please. Please help."

By Saturday, I knew we needed intervention. This couldn't be what the doctor expected to happen. Unsure of where else to turn, I called Dr. Miller's cellphone, explaining Ashley's behavior.

"Bring her to the ER. I will have them admit her to the oncology floor. You did the right thing by calling, David."

I do not remember a lot from those few days, but I do remember one thing – I did not want to die. Even as I endured the awful pain and heartbreak of cancer, I never thought about harming myself. I was shocked to hear David recount the past few days to me. I felt lost.

Because I had expressed suicidal thoughts, a psychiatrist came by to see me in the hospital. His white lab coat fell haphazardly over his thin shoulders, and his pointed brown shoes looked like boats poking out from below the hem of his gray slacks. An air of condescension seeped through his words before his eyes looked up from the chart long enough to meet mine.

"Have you ever had suicidal thoughts before?" He asked, launching into a string of scripted questions after a brief hello.

"Absolutely not." The force of my response hurled my words across the room like a boomerang.

As his line of questioning continued, I sensed he viewed me as a suicidal addict, which couldn't have been further from the truth. Our words volleyed back and forth as tension mounted in the room. He suggested a newer drug called Suboxone, which would provide similar benefits to Methadone, without the negative side effects. As a tightly controlled substance, he explained I would need to get the prescription from him, even Dr. Miller couldn't prescribe it. I told him I would consider it.

Much of the duration of the 48-hour hospital stay was spent at odds with the cocky, young psychiatrist. The tension climaxed one afternoon when he referred to me as an addict.

"Addicts in your situation can greatly benefit from Suboxone."

"Excuse me sir, I'm going to have to ask you to leave."

He stared blankly, first at me and then to David.

I fought to steady my voice as I locked my eyes with his. "Sir, for almost two years, I have been treated for cancer. I have followed every doctor's orders in regards to my medication. I am not an addict, and I refuse to be treated like one."

He shrugged his shoulders and turned to leave, letting the door slam behind him.

After talking with the oncology nurses, I began to gain some understanding of what was happening in my body. While I was not addicted to drugs in the same way a drug addict craves his next fix, my body had become dependent on the drugs in a similar way.

I left the hospital despondent, clutching a bottle of Suboxone in one hand and David's hand in the other. I had agreed to a few doses in the hospital, but felt uneasy about continuing to take it, fearing the same effects the Methadone had produced. It didn't seem to help the withdrawal symptoms at all, and a few quick Google searches over the next few days cemented my decision not to take it. It was a known habit-forming drug, and I didn't want to take the risk of becoming addicted to a medication that didn't even seem to be helping.

So, we were back at square one. At my next appointment, I reiterated to Dr. Miller that I wanted to stop the medication – cold turkey. Even calm and controlled Dr. Miller seemed to panic at my suggestion. However, two weeks into this detox ordeal, and more than eight weeks removed from my final maintenance chemo treatment, desperation had set in.

Anticipating her reaction, I had come up with a plan. "Put me in the hospital. Let me attempt the cold

242

turkey detox there, that way I can be closely monitored. I know I can do this. I want to do this."

Seeing my determination, she agreed to explore the possibility.

"The first hurdle will be the insurance company. In-patient detox would typically happen in a mental institution. If I admit you there, it will be on your record the rest of your life," she cautioned.

However, she agreed to go to bat for me with the insurance company, if I agreed to see an addiction psychologist before I attempted the detox. Fearing another encounter like the psychiatrist during my last hospital stay, I expressed reluctance, but eventually agreed. Dr. Miller's motherly firmness eclipsed even my own.

***

David filed behind me as we walked into Dr. Michael Gordon's office. The long brown leather couch along the wall fit the picture from the movies of what a psychologist's office would contain. A large, ornate stained desk, framed by two windows and two tall bookcases commanded the remaining space in the room. The rich burgundy leather chairs flanking the desk matched the rich red and gold flecked wall paper. I felt out of place in my denim capris and flip flops. Dr. Gordon's chair swung around as we moved further into the room.

"Well, hello there." His warm voice deflated the tension that had swelled inside me like a balloon. He ushered us into the two fancy chairs. "Tell me what brings you guys to me today."

As my story tumbled out, tears glistened in his eyes. When I finished, he reached in his coat pocket to pull out a white handkerchief and then dabbed his eyes. "You see, my wife died of cancer a few years ago. Horrible. Just horrible." He choked back sobs as he briefly recounted her story.

"So, I know all about the pain cancer patients have to endure. David, I feel for you, son. That's not an easy thing to watch your wife go through."

He leaned back, his chair rocking slightly as he stroked his chin. Then he pointed his finger as me, wagging it slightly. "I can tell you're a fighter. You fought that cancer and you won. If you feel like you can do this and agree to do it under medical supervision, I believe you can. I mean, it's not how I would do it, but then again, us guys can be wimps sometimes." He winked at David as he chuckled.

He walked me through what to expect and offered to answer any questions we had. As we stood and turned to leave, he handed me his card. "Just in case you ever need me in the future," but then he paused and winked again, "but I don't expect I will ever need to see you again."

His words bolstered my confidence. Feeling the weight of what I was about to endure, I whispered, "God, help me."

***

May 21, 2009

I walked through the familiar doors of the hospital at 8:00AM sharp. With Harley at David's parent's house, I focused on what I hoped would be the last major hurdle in my cancer journey. My paisley printed bag hung on David's shoulder as we rode the elevator to the oncology floor. My heart pounded in my chest as I feared the minor withdrawal symptoms I had experienced at home would pale in comparison to what awaited me over the next three days. Three days – we were told that was the magic number. If you could make it past day three, you would be on the downhill side of detox.

Just before noon, Dr. Miller walked over to my bed, placing her hands on my shoulder. "Are you sure you want to do this?"

"Absolutely," I said, surprised with how confident my words sounded.

The nurse walked in and pulled the patches from my back, the gel sticking and oozing as it peeled off. She pulled back my gown, administering one final dose of Dilaudid, to help ease the shock of removing the patches. I fumbled with the awkward hospital remote and flipped through channels on the TV, until finally landing on a house remodeling show. It felt like waiting for a time bomb to explode inside me.

As the beginning effects started to show, I prayed.

"Lord, I know You are with me. I know You will not leave me. Please help me. This feels like the valley of the shadow of death all over again. Help me to rest in You during this storm."

My phone beeped. I leaned across the crumpled bed linens to grab it from the rolling food tray situated at the end of my bed. Tears filled my eyes as I saw the picture flash across the screen. Harley stood in Patsy's garden, his blonde hair reflecting the bright spring sunshine. Across his tiny, outstretched finger sat a furry green and black caterpillar. Boyhood wonder shone in his eyes. I could hear his giggles as I pictured the furry creature inch up his hand and arm. I imagined the shock of the caterpillar as my tiny boy launched him through the air with glee as he shook his finger in excitement. I chuckled as I thought about how many caterpillars would end up in my house one day and marveled at the fact that I would be around to see that.

That little boy in the picture, grinning in his blue-striped overalls – he was my why. I had to endure this temporary pain in order to be the kind of mom I wanted to be for him. I didn't want to be chained to the power of medicine I no longer needed. I wanted to be free from the brain fog that had surrounded me for months. I needed to be free to be the mom I wanted to be for Harley and the wife I longed to be for David. I would need that picture in the coming days for motivation to keep going.

By early evening, the implosion had begun. Pain racked every inch of my body like a demon trying to tear me apart from the inside. It can only be accurately described as pure hell. My body dripped with sweat soaking through my hospital gown and sheets. I clutched my knees to my chest and curled up in a ball, desperate to find a position that eased the pain. An almost involuntary rocking motion surged through my body. David walked over and secured the rails hoping they would keep me from rocking myself out of the bed.

David: *I thought I had endured the worst when I saw her in the depths of cancer. I soon realized cancer was nothing compared to detox. I fought back waves of nausea as I once again had to watch my wife enduring unimaginable pain. I felt powerless to help her and wanted nothing more than to bear her pain in my body. It drew me close to the Lord as I imagined the pain of Jesus on the cross. Watching someone you love suffer puts the cross in such perspective. I did the only thing I could possibly do for my wife in that moment – I prayed. I begged God to spare her life and bring her through this. I never wanted her to have to experience pain again, not even a splinter. I slipped outside to get a cup of coffee when I could no longer hold my emotions inside. The faith that had blossomed in my heart over the last two years was being tested. I just wished for an easier way for all of this to be over.*

Krista: *I continued my nightly routine of calling to check on Ashley. In all my years of nursing, I had never seen a patient on as much pain medication as Ashley was on. Given that, I knew the detox process would be extremely difficult, despite her resolve. So, I was surprised when she answered the phone. She talked a million miles an hour at first, filling me in on everything that was going on. Then suddenly she stopped talking.*

My heart skipped a beat. Thankfully, just a moment later David picked up the phone before my mind had too long to wonder what had happened.

"Hello? Krista? Seems some of the medication kicked in."

She was basically unconscious for the next twenty-four hours. Detox is no joke.

By the third day, I started to emerge from the black hole of anguish. Seeing my improvement, David felt comfortable leaving me with my mom while he went to work. That afternoon, my hospital door opened and my little ray of sunshine toddled in. I smiled for the first time in three days. Patsy lifted Harley up onto my bed. He nestled his little sweaty head underneath my chin and patted my chest with his chubby little fist.

"Ma-ma!" His squeals brought delight to my heart. We snuggled for another minute, until he squirmed down, plopping his feet on the tile floor, ready to explore the new space. Eighteen-month-old boys don't stay in one place very long. After a few more minutes, Patsy collected Harley and his toys and turned to leave. I slipped my shoes on, feeling strong enough to walk them to the elevator.

I pressed my lips against his silky-smooth cheek. "I love you sweet boy. Momma loves you. I'll be home soon."

As the elevator doors closed, I collapsed into a puddle of tears on the floor right there in the hallway. My raw emotions burst through into a full blown ugly cry. That little boy had only known a sick mom, laid up in hospital beds and recliners. I felt like he deserved a better mom, a healthier mom that could run and play with him at the park. Leaving a puddle of tears on the tile in the hallway, I prayed that, with God's help, that would be exactly the kind of mom I would be for him one day.

Chapter 21
Baby Prayers

"Call unto me and I will answer thee, and shew thee great and mighty things,
which thou knowest not." Jeremiah 33:3

David: *The concrete path stretched beyond my view as my tires hummed along the dotted yellow line. Following my buddy and fellow firefighter's line, I coasted down a narrow strip of hill, anticipating another rolling climb a few hundred feet away. Mike and I had the crazy idea to bike the twenty-three miles to work our rookie year. Over the next several years, when the weather cooperated, as it rarely does during May through August in Georgia, we parked our trucks at the nearest Silver Comet Entry point and got a quick workout in. Sure beat sitting in Atlanta traffic.*

The strip of straight trail gave my brain margin to drift as I sped along, my knees rising and falling in a predictable rhythm. Ashley's two-year remission anniversary had just passed the week before and I reflected on the flurry of events that followed. With each clear scan, we breathed a heavy sigh of relief. Dr. Miller told us five years would be a big milestone. At five years, the survival rate would increase significantly. Until then, we just continued to pray for the best and trust the Lord.

It took Ashley almost a full year to finish the detox process and truly be free of any withdrawal symptoms. I had no idea her body had become so dependent on those drugs. I stood in awe once again at my wife's tenacity and determination to overcome such an enormous obstacle. As the months passed, though, I could see another struggle brewing in her heart.

She wanted another baby. This was familiar territory. After her surgery, she flung us down a risky path of fertility treatments in an attempt to harvest her eggs. Seeing her devastation when it failed left me with an enormous pile of guilt. I should have said no. I should have protected her from herself. I wanted so desperately to give her what she wanted, but more than anything I just wanted her. Another baby meant nothing to me if it meant I had to lose her to get it.

The ache in her heart may have been the same two years later, but her approach was radically different. I could see the Lord rebuild her faith as He rebuilt her body. She had a sense of calm that she didn't have before. I think it was trust. Somewhere in her darkest moments, she had released the grip of control she thought she had and as the popular song says, cried, "Jesus, take the wheel!"

In the summer of 2010, we really began discussing the possible options for having another child. We started where we should have started the time before – we prayed. For months we just prayed. We asked God for wisdom to know His plan for our family, for what path we should take and submitted our hearts to be willing to hear an answer we may not like.

When mentioning the possibility of carrying another child to my doctors, you would have thought I was asking to fire a nuclear weapon in my living room.

Dr. Miller: "No, definitely not. No more babies."

Dr. Parks: "Absolutely not. Don't even entertain the thought."

Dr. Soundararajan: "One hundred percent, no."

Because the type of cancer I had was never determined, no one could be sure what brought it on. If hormones from Harley's pregnancy had fueled my cancer, everyone agreed that having another baby could possibly ignite the fire again. Understanding the risks and the concern, I listened to their advice.

Not wanting to give up on the dream of having more children though, David and I began looking into adoption. I spent months researching agencies and talking to friends who had adopted children before. My health posed the biggest obstacle for adoption. We had no idea if an agency would even entertain placing a child with someone who had had stage-four cancer and currently had a 75-90 percent chance of recurrence. It didn't seem likely, but we had just seen God perform the impossible. I took comfort in the fact that if God intended for us to have another baby, He would provide a way.

In the fall of 2010, more health roadblocks slowed any discussion of future children. I began experiencing episodes where my heart would start racing uncontrollably for no apparent reason. At first I wrote it off as nothing, but as the episodes became more frequent, my concern grew. After a swollen lymph node turns out to be stage four cancer, it is somewhat understandable to become a bit of a hypochondriac. I tried to get David to feel my pulse, but he never seemed to be around at the moment the episodes would hit.

After a few weeks, I went to see a cardiologist to ease my concern. He gave me a heart monitor to wear, but at first, it detected nothing unusual. Then one night, as we had just laid down in bed, it happened again.

"David! It's happening! Feel my pulse!"

He shot up in the bed in a typical firefighter response. He reached over, grabbed my wrist and pressed his finger along the bone just below my thumb.

David: The first two beats were rhythmic, but then it would pause, skipping a beat. As the heart starting beating again, it was as if it was trying to catch up – the next several beats would be significantly faster. As a trained EMT, I knew enough to know she needed medical attention.

"We need to go to the ER, now," David replied, leaping out of bed to get dressed. Despite my many ER visits and hospitalizations, I knew those words didn't come lightly from David. Normally someone had to be losing a limb or literally on the verge of dying before David would suggest an ER visit. Within twenty minutes, my mom stood in my living room to stay with Harley, and we rushed out the door.

At the ER, an EKG revealed the problem that had eluded my cardiologist before.

"You have SVT – Supraventricular Tachycardia. Which basically means you have an electrical short in your heart, causing it to misfire. Given your history, it could have been caused by your chemotherapy treatments," the doctor explained. He instructed me to follow up with my cardiologist the following week.

As the episodes became more frequent, my cardiologist noticed irregularities on my monitor, one night my heartrate spiked to over 200 beats per minute. At my next appointment, my cardiologist discussed my options moving forward: medication or a heart ablation. We agreed that the best course of action would be the ablation, which would be a minor procedure to take out the small, defective part of the heart.

Two weeks later, I sat in the same waiting room and maybe even the same chair that I had two years earlier. The automatic doors shuffled quietly with the hustle and bustle of a busy hospital. Each time they slid open, a wave of warm, humid air wafted inside. Harley, oblivious to my inner turmoil, sat next to me. He wiggled down my legs, stretching his white tennis shoes toward the floor. *Plop*. My face winced as his chubby little hands hit the orange carpet. While it appeared clean, I imagined the hospital floor must be crawling with germs. He had already been sitting for an hour at the cardiologist's office earlier in the day. Two-year-old boys don't enjoy sitting – especially not quietly. I tried to entertain him and keep my mind off my surroundings. My hand rhythmically stroked his blonde hair as I watched the minutes tick by on the clock above the door. I noticed his jeans hit just above his ankles; time to put those in the ever-growing pile for Goodwill.

Nearby, a young girl with blonde pigtails eagerly pushed a book into her mother's hands. The woman eased the girl into her lap, brushing the ponytails aside to read the words on the page. A husband and wife behind me whispered quietly, working out a plan for dinner. She mentioned Mexican, but he wanted to try a new Chinese restaurant in the next town over. Hunger pains gripped my stomach as I listened.

It had been a long afternoon. It had been a long two years. I thrive on having a plan, on being in control; but the past two years had been a whirlwind of the unexpected. I clung to the fragments of life I could control, which were few and far between more often than not. Today was supposed to be different. I knew the plan for today – my appointment with the cardiologist to discuss my upcoming heart ablation, a quick trip to the hospital for paperwork and pre-op blood work, a stop by the bank, and then home to put Harley down for a nap. Monday afternoon naps are quiet and peaceful – my reset from the weekend and busy Sundays at church. With my eyelids struggling to stay open, I planned to steal a nap with him today.

"Ashley Hallford!"

I jumped at the sound of my own name as a nurse in blue scrubs called from the doorway. I gathered Harley and his collection of cars and followed the nurse down the hallway, her eyes never leaving the chart in her hand. The lines on the floor seemed to lead us like an ill-fated treasure map. Harley toddled along behind her, clutching a yellow and blue striped car too precious to put in the bag with these others.

As I turned the corner, a wave of emotions floated through my body, enveloping me as I paused in the doorway. This was the room where it all began with sixteen biopsy needles and no anesthesia. My feet felt like chunks of cement; they wouldn't budge. The drab walls were still pale yellow and in desperate need of cheerful artwork or something to brighten the space. I gripped my chest with my hand as the tidal wave of emotions burst through my weak attempt to suppress them. Two years had not been long enough to forget the physical and emotional pain of that day.

Glancing up from her chart, the nurse's eyes briefly met mine, probably unsure of what kept me standing in the doorway like a statue. I was there for routine, pre-op blood work. A quick needle prick and two vials of blood and it would be over. She couldn't possibly have known the source of my distress. She shifted her supplies and made small talk with Harley in an attempt to give me a moment to relax.

"You ready, honey?"

I took a deep breath – forcing myself to regain my composure. The needle pierced my vein; I didn't flinch. After everything I had endured, I barely felt the prick of the needle anymore. Harley's wiggling had stopped as he sat mesmerized by the nurse's quick, efficient movements, his big eyes following her every move.

It was as if time stopped for those few moments. As I held my son I thought about all that had happened – much of it in this hospital – since that day. The depths of sorrow and the height of joy were impossible to grasp. My husband, David, and I had walked through a storm like none we had ever imagined and sitting there, I relived it all at high speed.

I was abruptly roused from my thoughts.

"You're all done. Have a good day."

The nurse turned her back as she deposited the needle into the bin on the wall. I gathered Harley and stood up, steadying myself on the arm of the chair with Harley's little hand firmly in mine and his little round face and blue eyes looking intently up at my own face. I gave him a weak smile as I brushed the final tear away.

As I walked out of the room, I uttered a feeble "Thank you" as my feet rushed to put distance between me and that room.

Maybe the thank you was to the nurse, or maybe it was more of a prayer. So much uncertainty still swirled around me, but as I walked farther down the hallway, my sorrow melted into gratitude. God had given me far more than I had ever deserved. Tears rolled down my cheeks again as I thanked Him for His sovereign goodness in my life. Even if I didn't live another day, the past two years with my husband and son were simply a gift no one ever thought I would live to see.

***

The following Monday I counted the grooves in the square ceiling tiles as I lay waiting for the heart ablation to begin. The original intent during the procedure was for me to be awake but drugged enough to keep me in a "twilight" state. I needed to be awake enough during the procedure in order to communicate with the doctor. Given all the medication I had been on in the past, I warned them that the minor-league drugs they had in mind, probably wouldn't affect me in the same way they did other patients. The staff in the room kept staring at me, waiting for the drugs to kick in.

"Wow, you weren't kidding," the nurse commented as I lay wide awake ten minutes into the process. While I didn't experience any pain, the procedure felt a bit unnerving. In order to locate the defective area, my heart rate was increased incrementally until it raced beyond anything I had ever felt before. My body vibrated along the table as if I were riding on a hummingbird's wings.

As we walked out of the hospital that afternoon, I wondered if this would finally be the last step in the cancer

258

journey. I wanted to push toward a happier, swaddle-wrapped and squishy-cheeks kind of dream.

***

By the spring of 2011, normalcy had returned to our family. At three-and-a-half, Harley filled our days with plenty of running, jumping, choo-choo trains, and of course fire trucks. I finally felt like a normal young mom. We spent our days playing with friends, making crafts, and reading books. As the only grandchild on either side of the family, Harley received plenty of love and attention, but I started to sense a loneliness in his little heart.

"Mama, am I going to have a baby sister one day?" he blurted out one night as he crawled into bed. Our group of friends had all had babies about the same time I had Harley. By now all of them either had another child or were expecting. I guess, like Adam did in the Garden, Harley realized he was alone. Sadness seized my heart as I formed my response.

"Well, Harley, I'm not sure." I paused to gather my thoughts and keep my emotions under control. "God gives people babies, so I guess all we can do is pray and ask God and see what He says."

I could not have imagined the impact my words would have on a tender little three-year-old's heart. Harley began praying for a baby after that conversation and not just any baby – a sister. Every meal and bedtime prayer included his heartfelt plea for a baby sister. His Sunday School teacher even came to us one Sunday after church.

"We started to pray before class this morning and Harley stopped me," she began. "He insisted that I pray for him to have a baby sister."

"Well I guess he knows the right person to ask, because it would take a miracle to make that happen!" David chuckled in response.

Wherever we happened to be, Harley was relentless in his petition. As most kids do, Harley had one volume when talking – loud. At a restaurant one night, Harley asked to pray over the food.

"Thank you for this food and please, *please* give me a baby sister now." His voice carried to all the surrounding tables. An older couple behind us chuckled as the old man gave us a slight nod, as if to say, "Well, what are you waiting on?" Obviously that man didn't need to hear our life story and the complications facing having another child, so we just smiled and turned away, trying to bury ourselves in the basket of breadsticks.

Health issues continued to plague me and forced us to push the idea of another baby further down the road. My throat had never fully healed from the effects of the intense radiation, and by September of that year, eating had becoming increasingly difficult. I would frequently choke on food, and even swallowing felt precarious at times. My doctors recommended having my esophagus stretched, which would help alleviate my symptoms.

"Will that fix the problem?" I asked, dreading another surgery.

"It is hard to know. Due to the damage from the radiation, you may have to have this procedure periodically for the rest of your life."

Before leaving the office, I scheduled the procedure for the following Friday. I pulled my sunglasses down from my head and reached in my purse for my phone as I ambled through the parking lot. The first cool breezes of fall whispered through the air, bringing relief from the long, blistering days of summer. My phone buzzed before I could dial my mom's number, as if she could sense that I was about to call. I briefly explained the procedure as I listened to sounds of Harley playing in the background.

"It is scheduled for next Friday," I reported, climbing into the car.

"*Next* Friday? Ashley, are you sure? Will you feel better in time to go to the beach?"

Our entire family had a beach trip planned, leaving the following Saturday. That would give me a full week to recover. "Mom, the surgeon said I would be fine after just a couple days. The beach will be fine. Don't worry."

David: *The morning of that surgery felt all too familiar. I waved goodbye to Harley and drove Ashley to the hospital; however, leaving a running, bouncing almost four-year old in my mom's living room felt significantly easier than leaving a sickly premature baby in an isolette at the hospital. As with previous procedures, we were told that this would be a quick and easy one, lasting less than thirty minutes. I barely had time to grab a cup of coffee before a nurse called me back to see Ashley.*

As they rolled me into the recovery room, stabbing pains filled my chest. The nurse stood at the corner of my bed. My eyes wandered to the right and landed on the surgeon. He strolled over as the nurse moved in to check my vitals.

"How's everything feeling?" he asked.

"Actually, my chest hurts, like sharp stabbing pains."

With my words, his shoulders drooped and his eyes widened. It took a minute for my brain to process what my eyes were seeing. Panic. His eyes screamed: panic.

"She needs a CT scan, now!"

As my bed whirled down the hallway, I turned toward the nurse steering the bed from my right side.

"A CT, for what? What's going on?" The flurry of activity seemed to drown out my words. As we careened into the room, I tapped the nurse's arm. "Excuse me, what is going on?"

"The doctor needs to take a look and see what is going on in your chest to cause your pain," she explained.

As she fumbled through a drawer, I overlooked her simple response to press a more urgent matter.

"Ma'am, I am allergic to the contrast dye." Her hand waved slightly as if she were brushing away a pesky

262

fly. Minutes later with a needle in my arm, I barked my words again.

"Ma'am! I said I am allergic to the contrast dye."

"Oh, well, this is what the doctor ordered," she replied, seemingly unfazed by my revelation. However, minutes later, red hives erupted on my abdomen and arms like fire ants at a Sunday picnic. My throat, which was already in rough shape, swelled, making talking and breathing difficult. The flurry of activity multiplied as Benadryl and steroids were administered to combat the allergic reaction. The CT procedure resumed once the reaction subsided. The nurse avoided my annoyed gaze as I slid onto the table.

"Unfortunately, during the procedure, a perforation of your esophagus occurred," the doctor explained once I had been wheeled back to my room. "This is allowing pockets of air to collect in your chest cavity." His brown tussled hair receded deeply above his temples, and his olive skin stood in contrast to the baby blue collared shirt standing just above his white coat. He paced awkwardly at the end of the bed, like a caged house cat.

David and I both sat speechless, exchanging glances between each other and the surgeon. I figured yelling at them wouldn't benefit anyone and would probably just hurt my throat more, so I sat in quiet annoyance, ruminating over the bungled series of events. Once again, Murphy's Law seemed to be in full swing where it concerned my medical procedures – anything that can go wrong, will go wrong.

Sensing my emotional frustration and physical pain, he excused himself briefly, the door creaking behind him as he left. His voiced carried through the crevice though.

"Clear my schedule. Yes, cancel all my appointments."

He waded through the thick air of frustration in the room and perched himself beside my bed. He picked my hand up and held it gingerly, patting it in a fatherly sort of way. I'm not sure who needed more comfort in that moment – me or him.

David: *After the comedy of errors at my wife's expense, I soon took matters into my own hands. As a side job, I worked a few shifts a month with a local ambulance company. After a couple phone calls and a short wait, I loaded Ashley up and took her to the hospital across town where her cancer surgery had been performed. She had been through enough; the old country hospital could practice on someone else's wife.*

As the ambulance barreled down the road, jostling with every bump and turn, my mom's words echoed in my mind: the beach. "I may have to eat my words on that one," I muttered to myself, unsure if this situation could be resolved in time to make the trip or not.

With a fresh set of doctors and nurses, my situation was assessed and a plan of action took shape.

"Best case scenario would be that the tear in your esophagus would heal on its own in four or five days," the doctor explained, resting his hands on the side rail of my bed.

"And worst case scenario…" I posed, not really sure I wanted to know the answer.

"Well, worst case would be going in to repair the tear, which would be an extensive surgery. Let's just hope for the best and see what happens," he continued. "You will not be able to eat or drink anything while we wait for the tear to heal. We will repeat the scan in five days and reevaluate the situation then."

I sighed. No Frappuccinos this time. No fluffy whipped cream.

Thankfully Murphy's Law didn't extend its reach further into the week. When the scans were repeated on Wednesday, the tear appeared to be healed. We thanked the Lord for His graciousness again knowing that despite the inconvenience of the situation, it could have been much worse had the perforation not healed on its own.

After being discharged just after 1:00PM on Thursday, David and I rushed home. In a flurry of suitcases, flip flops, and sunscreen, we packed for a week at the beach. Despite having been in the hospital all week, I worked furiously on Friday afternoon and evening to clean my house. We were scheduled to leave before breakfast on Saturday, and I could not stand the thought of leaving a dirty house behind.

As we stuck our toes in the sand on Saturday, I couldn't believe we had actually made it. I insisted on a few beach pictures before Harley ran to play in the sand. Despite the fact that we all felt a bit haggard, the pictures turned out to be some of my favorites. If I had to endure an unintentional five-day fast, at least my swimsuit got to reap the temporary rewards.

My mom chuckled as I collapsed into the beach chair, my sunglasses hanging on the end of my nose.

"Don't even say 'I told you so,'" I joked, pressing my eyes closed as the sun warmed my cheeks. "I couldn't have possibly known all that was going to happen."

Chapter 22
Search for a Surrogate

*"Be careful for nothing; but in everything by prayer
and supplication with thanksgiving let your
requests be made known unto God." Phil. 4:6*

After returning home from the beach trip, our focus returned once again to having more children. We continued to pray for the Lord's direction, unsure of the next step to take, with adoption or surrogacy looking like the only two possible options. Harley, still unrelenting in his prayer campaign, felt sure the Lord would answer his request soon.

It is strange how the Lord orchestrates events, even in the midst of capris and tunics in the ladies' department at Target. Harley and I had run into the store with a short list, but as is often the case, found ourselves wandering through aisles not on our list. My phone buzzed alerting me to a message. I had posted on Facebook asking if anyone knew any surrogates. I knew it was a long shot but figured it was worth a try.

David and I had just decided the week before that surrogacy seemed like the best fit for our family. I had even mentioned the idea to Dr. Miller, who favored surrogacy far above trying to carry a baby myself. However, given that I didn't really have anyone in mind who would be able to loan her body to me for nine months, it seemed like a dead end.

Yet, I stood in Target, looking at my phone, stunned at what seemed to be God's answer to prayer. A friend replied to my post, saying she just happened to have the name of a woman who she felt would be perfect for the job. I immediately replied to get more information, feeling like the Lord was planting a new seed of hope in my desperate heart.

What I envisioned would be an awkward introduction, (Hi, I'm Ashley. I know we've never met, but would you have my baby for me?), turned out to be more like meeting an old friend. Our phone conversations felt warm and familiar. I felt at ease knowing she would possibly carry our child. Only a few weeks passed from the Target conversation to sitting around a quaint table at a café on the north side of Atlanta discussing the finer details of how the surrogacy process would work between us.

With a hesitant approval from Dr. Miller, I called Dr. Fogle's office, the fertility doctor that had helped us with the failed fertility cycle after my cancer surgery. They walked me through the first few steps in the surrogacy process. Almost feeling the warm snuggles of a newborn in my arms, I wanted to plunge in and get started right away. I snagged the first available appointments, and consultations, paperwork and rounds of blood work ensued for Candie, David, and me over the next two months. If the bloodwork came back fine, then I would start a round of fertility treatments to stimulate egg production. The dose would be lower than it had been during the fertility treatments after my cancer surgery. Since I wasn't trying to harvest a larger quantity of eggs to freeze, less hormones would be needed to produce a few eggs to be used in the IVF process.

Weeks later, while sitting in front of the tree with Harley on Christmas morning, I dreamed with anticipation about what our family would look like the following Christmas. The blood work for Candie and David looked good as we anticipated moving into the next phase of the process. As usual though, my body seemed to continue its uncooperative spirit. My AMH levels, a hormone that acts as an indicator to fertility, came back slightly lower than the ideal range. Dr. Fogle explained that while a low AMH level could indicate decreased ovarian store reserves, we could continue to move forward with the process, while monitoring the hormone level.

Time between appointments crawled. During the day, I cherished being a mom to Harley as we stacked blocks and read books, but as my head hit the pillow each night, the ache to be a mom to a baby I had never met swelled in my soul. I cried out to God daily in anticipation of a dream I couldn't grasp.

"Lord, you know my desire for another baby. You gave me the most precious, perfect little boy a mom could ask for. I am so thankful for him and I would be content if he were the only one. I know many women don't even have the blessing of one baby. Sometimes I feel selfish even asking for more, but You know my heart. You made it. You knit this desire to be a mom into the very fabric of my being. I can't imagine what it would be like to hold my baby without sickness and doctors pressing in on every side. Between surgeries, hospital stays, medication fog, and relentless pain, I feel like I missed so much of the first two years of Harley's life. If You choose to give us a baby, I long for brighter, happier days to relish the joy of a new life without death lurking at the door.

"Between my battered body, financial strain, emotional roller coasters, and a high probability of recurrence, this dream seems impossible. But then, that's who You are. You are the God of the impossible. Not just for Moses and Abraham, but for me. You graciously chose to heal me when so many other people die. I have no idea why. Even when I pushed and clawed to fight the battle on my own, You didn't leave me. Like a Father watching his little kid put on a suit of armor and clumsily walk around with the confidence to fight the giant, despite tripping on her own feet, You let me swing the sword around for a little bit until it wore me out. Then in my helpless desperation I finally let go enough to allow my faith to grow. I began to trust in You more than myself, so slowly at first that I almost didn't notice.

"Now years later, I can look back and see I never really had the reigns of control I thought were branded with my name. This time is different. I know that You are in control and I'm so thankful for it. I'm thankful that the burden of decision and merit doesn't rest on my frail shoulders. I am thankful that all You ask me to do is trust you. As David wrote in Psalms, 'Delight yourself in the Lord and He will give you the desires of your heart.' You obviously know how much I want a baby, but I can honestly say I want You more. I delight in a loving Father that has saved me from something so much worse than cancer – my sin.

"So, I'm just going to leave this bundle of my heart right here, like Hannah did. Whatever you choose to do with it, I trust You and I know that You are good."

Monday, February 13, 2012

Dr. Fogle pulled her chair close to the enormous desk, her blonde hair pulled into a tight bun along her neckline. Her perfectly manicured nails gripped the chart as she peered over the information. Her eyes lifted to meet mine. I had seen that look before. I reached for David's hand between the rails of the chair.

"Ashley, I'm so sorry, but I cannot in good faith continue in this process."

We had just walked across the hallway from an internal ultrasound. I've learned it's impossible to accurately decipher someone's face as they read an x-ray or an ultrasound. It always seems terrible. Her pause, the length of her sighs, the downward tilt of her head, all screamed that bad news would follow. Waves of sadness battered me as I fought to hold it together as she continued.

"Your AMH levels are low, which indicate that you are in the early stages of menopause, most likely due to your cancer treatments. The ultrasound I just performed confirmed what the test results indicate - you have no eggs in reserve. Even with hormone stimulation, the process of you producing any eggs for us to harvest would be impossible. It is incredibly difficult under the best of circumstances. I cannot continue with this cycle knowing that there would be virtually no chance of success. I'm so sorry."

Tears dripped down my nose as the weight of the news sank into my soul. She encouraged us to look into adoption, even walking us through what that would look like and what to expect. I struggled to process her words, as if I had suddenly been locked in a sound proof case, only able to see her lips moving. We thanked her for her time and most of all, her honesty. Bad news now seemed at least a little better than bad news further down the road.

As we reached the car, the dam started to break. I jerked the door handle and collapsed into the seat, letting the door slam behind me as I pulled my boots from the threshold just in time. I soaked the shoulder of David's long-sleeve Georgia Bulldogs t-shirt. His tears fell silently on my head as we sat fixed in the front seat of the car, the engine purring to keep the chilly February air at bay.

The silence hung in the air as David navigated our way back home, leaving our dreams in a pile of rubble in the parking lot.

"This is where the rubber meets the road of your faith," I thought staring out the window. God had clearly closed to door to biological children. My emotions raged within me to fight and kick down the door with a sledge hammer. Maybe another doctor – a second opinion, but my panic soon subsided.

"No. Lord, I trust you. Whatever you are doing, whatever this means for us, I trust that you have a plan for our little family." I breathed the prayers silently through my lips. Maybe adoption was the answer, or maybe we were just supposed to have Harley. I could only be sure of one thing – God had a plan and all I needed to do was sit back and watch it unfold.

The next morning, I rolled out of bed, and stumbled to the coffee pot as Harley bounced down the stairs. Valentine's Day plans were in the works with homemade valentines and cookies waiting to be made. First, however, I had to go to the hospital for pre-op blood work ahead of another esophagus dilation scheduled for the following Monday. I cringed as I recalled the debacle of the last procedure and prayed Monday's would be different.

Our family seemed to be on a never-ending carousel of medical procedures. Before my procedure on Monday, Harley was scheduled to have a wart removed on Thursday. As a little guy, Harley's mouth acted as his antenna to the world. Everywhere we went, he constantly put his mouth on things – store windows, shopping carts, fruit displays, and yes, even a floor or two on occasion. Despite my best efforts to thwart this pattern, his silly little grin would inevitably end up plastered on a germ covered surface multiple times a day.

I knew one day the disgusting habit would catch up with him. He developed a wart on his lip. Normally a wart would be simple to remove in a dermatologist's office, but of course with our family, nothing can be easy. Because of the placement of the wart, our dermatologist recommended we take him to a plastic surgeon to have it removed to minimize scarring.

Devastating news from the ultrasound on Monday, lab work on Tuesday, Harley's wart removal on Thursday, and my throat procedure on the following Monday certainly didn't put us in the running for preferred customers with our insurance company.

Thursday morning, we walked through the doors of the children's hospital where Harley had been hospitalized for RSV as a baby. I glanced at Dr. Spector's office across the street and whispered a prayer thanking God that on most days, I was no longer the patient. I flashed back to the day my mom helped me stumble across the street to his office. I still couldn't believe all that had happened in the last four and a half years.

My parents and David's parents joined us in the waiting room. Given my history, even the smallest medical event carries more weight than for other people. When they informed us that the procedure was complete, we gathered our stuff and filed out into the hallway. Moments later, the doors slid open and his bed rolled out. Harley's body looked so small, even in the kid-sized bed. My hand swept his hair back as I stroked his face and kissed his cheeks. He whined and curled his body from side to side. I glanced at the nurse on the other side of his bed.

"It is normal for him to be a bit irritable as the anesthesia wears off. Everything went well and he will be ready to go home in a few hours," she commented as she continued to wheel his bed toward the recovery room.

As we walked, my phone vibrated in my purse. Given the situation, I battled the urge to ignore it, but glanced down to see who it was. It was my surgeon's office. Not wanting to miss potentially important information about Monday's surgery, I shuffled to the side of the hallway and answered the phone, waving to David that I would catch up with them.

"Hi Ashley, it's Dr. Smith's office."

I clicked the heel of my boots impatiently along the dull tile floor as I anticipated a routine scheduling reminder that had momentarily suspended my caring for my son: surgery Monday, got it.

"There seems to be a problem with your pre-op blood work," she began, her hesitation accented by brief pauses between each word.

My limbs froze, my heel stopped in mid-air just above the ground. This was it. The dreaded news that the cancer was back. In that split second, my thoughts screamed louder than her words on the other end of the phone. A hint of cheerfulness coated her voice as she continued.

"Ashley, the lab work says that you're pregnant."

275

Instantly my ballooning fear of cancer deflated, as confusion and disbelief surged to take its place.

"That's impossible. I can't get pregnant. I'm not pregnant. I just had an ultrasound four days ago. An internal ultrasound by a fertility specialist. She said I was in menopause." My conveyer belt of objections was halted as she fought to interrupt me.

"I understand. It was probably a mix up at the lab. We will need to repeat the labs as soon as possible to get this cleared up before your scheduled surgery on Monday."

"I can't today, my son just had surgery. Would tomorrow be too late?" I asked, wiping my suddenly sweaty palms against my jeans.

"That's fine. We will put the order in for stat labs, so we should have the results by the end of the day."

The receiver clicked as I stood in the hallway that had become a pit of quicksand. I stood staring at the stock photos lining the hallway across from me as I tried to process the news she had just shared. After a few moments, I shook myself, pulled my feet out of their suspended stance and headed back toward Harley, attempting to convince myself that it was a mistake. Twinges of guilt surfaced as I fought to press down waves of excitement.

"If it's true, should I be excited? But it's not true. There is no way. Dr. Fogle would have seen something on the ultrasound. It's a mix up. But what if it's not." My thoughts bantered back and forth like ping pong balls in a game with Forrest Gump.

I yanked David into the hallway, out of earshot of Harley and our parents.

"The lab work says I'm pregnant," I divulged in the best whisper I could manage given the substance of the news.

"Lab work, what lab work? Dr. Fogle's?" I relayed my conversation from moments before, but didn't allow much room for speculation.

"It has to be a mix up. There is no way I could be pregnant after what Dr. Fogle said at our appointment on Monday." My words sounded decisive, but I looked to his eyes for reassurance.

"Well, let's just see what they say tomorrow," David concluded, as calm and collected as ever.

We walked back to Harley's side with the bulging developments stuffed awkwardly between our lips. As we piled in the elevator, after Harley's discharge, I nudged David's arm. He didn't seem to notice as we shuffled six adults, Harley's wheelchair, and our escort into the space. I nudged harder. I spoke in a language only wives seem to understand – laser beam eyes. I even motioned with my hands, desperate to know if we should tell our parents the news or wait. Sensing the elevator ride would end before David's slow interpretation of my frantic sign language concluded, I took a deep breath.

"The surgeon's office called and the lab work says I'm pregnant."

The blurted words seemed to bounce around the room like a pinball machine. The wheelchair escort rolled his ankles nervously, I'm sure feeling like he had suddenly crashed an awkward, private party. As we funneled out of the elevator, our parents encircled me, each displaying varying degrees of shock across their faces.

Then the rapid-fire questions ensued.

"What?!?" "Are you sure?" "I thought that was impossible." "Did you talk to Dr. Miller?" "Is it safe for you and the baby?"

Talking over the crowd, I tried to squash the emotions, assuring everyone it had to be a mistake.

"Dr. Fogle would have noticed I was pregnant on Monday. It has to be a mix up with the blood work. They are going to repeat everything tomorrow." While their suspense lingered, mine faded that night as I went to bed, firmly convinced it would be silly to believe something that was simply impossible.

I marched in to the lab at 7:30 the next morning, anxious to get the results and put this excitement to rest. Three hours later, standing in my kitchen, my phone rang. I leaned against the counter as I pressed it to my ear. The same nurse from the day before was on the line.

"Ashley, I think you need to call your fertility doctor," she began with a chuckle, "because you are still pregnant." She expressed congratulations and let me know my throat surgery would obviously have to be canceled.

I stood speechless. God had once again done the impossible. I dropped to my knees right there in my kitchen, tears streaming down my face.

"God, I don't deserve this. Cured from an incurable cancer. A healthy baby at 32 weeks. Now a baby in a body that defies all medical odds. I don't know why You choose to give me such good gifts, but I am humbled and thankful for them. Protect this precious baby you placed inside of me."

I paused as I uttered a bold prayer that I wasn't sure I deserved to ask, "Just let this time be different."

Elation turned to dread as my doctors' faces flashed through my mind. I swallowed hard as I realized I would have to tell them. Only three and a half years into remission, I was sure this news would not be met with jubilation. Pushing that thought from my mind, I walked upstairs to share the news with David.

David: *While I was certainly happy about a baby, the concern for Ashley cast a shadow on that joy. I wasn't really shocked honestly, despite what we had been told just days before. I had watched God snatch my wife from the jaws of death, why should I be surprised if He gave us a baby when it seemed impossible. It reminded me of the lesson I learned watching her battle cancer – all I could do was pray. If her cancer had been fueled by hormones as they suggested, this pregnancy would be a breeding ground for it to come back. I prayed, knowing that since God had given us this baby, then He had a plan.*

After I called my mom, I called Dr. Fogle's office to make an appointment for the following week. As we walked into the office, we were immediately marched to the ultrasound room. Dr. Fogle sat in disbelief as the outline of a tiny baby appeared on the screen.

"There is no medical explanation for this. We performed an ultrasound and bloodwork last Monday and you were definitely not pregnant then. I just have no explanation."

David and I grinned at each other as I replied, "Well, we do. Evidently, God wanted us to have a baby the old-fashioned way!"

A smile broke out across her face as she nodded her head in apparent agreement. She congratulated us and wished us luck with the pregnancy. As we walked out of her office, I was struck that we would probably never be there again. Despite a kind, knowledgeable and willing staff, the office had been the scene of devastating heartbreak for us. God had not given me what I had so desperately wanted at the time, because He knew His ways were better than my own. I realized that had the egg harvest been successful, I would have missed out on the incredible blessing of this baby and more importantly, seeing the Lord's hand in our lives. For the first time, I was thankful for my cancer. I didn't want to repeat it, and I certainly wished things could have been different, but for the first time I began to see that God taught me things and grew my faith through cancer in ways I never expected.

Mixed emotions ran high as we shared the news with close family and friends. My doctors were understandably concerned. The options for scans evaporated with the confirmed pregnancy, so they would have to monitor my progress blindly. In addition to my regular OB appointments, I had to see a high-risk OB as well. Combined with visits to Dr. Miller, I was seen by a doctor two to three times a month throughout much of the pregnancy. We called it, "the most watched pregnancy ever."

As I approached the end of my first trimester, anticipation grew for finding out the gender. With no complications or signs of recurrence popping up, I could relish the excitement. It was no secret that while we were thankful for a baby and a healthy pregnancy, we were all hoping for a girl. On David's side of the family it had been 35 years since a girl had been born into the family. They were long overdue for some pink! Given the circumstances, I knew this baby would round out our family, and I dreamed of bows and frills for our little caboose.

Harley's prayer campaign had not ended when I found out I was pregnant. He continued to pray one specific prayer – he wanted a sister. He named the baby Flower, and I grew slightly concerned about his level of disappointment if he discovered he had a little brother on the way.

Given the high-risk nature of my pregnancy, I had an ultrasound virtually every appointment. When I was just fourteen weeks, I asked the tech if she could tell the gender.

"I think I can, but it is too early to give any solid information."

My heart skipped a beat! We were desperate to know if it was a boy or girl! How could she know and not share the news? She wrote her guess on the back of my chart.

"At your next appointment in two weeks, I'll let you know if my guess was right."

I fought back frustration as we left the appointment. Two weeks seemed like an eternity to wait, especially knowing that someone else knew. I wondered if it would be another boy, assuming boys are easier to identify at such an early stage than girls. Ultimately however, I knew any healthy baby would be a joy to our family and prayed the next fourteen days would pass quickly.

Two weeks later, David, Harley and I went back for the much-anticipated appointment. The ultrasound tech knew our story and how desperately Harley had been praying for a baby girl. David stood beside me as I reclined on the table, my tan flip flops peeking above my slightly raised stomach. Harley's little legs dangled above the ground, swishing back and forth in anticipation. He wore a blue striped shirt and gray shorts with his favorite tennis shoes.

"Mr. Harley, I hear that you have been hoping for a baby sister," the tech began as she spread the warm gel over my stomach.

"Yes, ma'am. I pray every day," he boldly replied, grinning from ear to ear.

As she glided the wand back and forth, snapping images for the doctor to review, she paused, smiled and looked right at Harley.

"Well, it looks you are going to have a little flower!"

Chapter 23
Walls of Grace

---

*"Now unto Him that is able to do exceeding
abundantly above all that we ask or think..."*
Eph. 3:20

Harley jumped to his feet in excitement, joyous giggles bubbling over. David and I both started crying. The simplistic joy and exhilaration of that moment were unparalleled in our lives up until that point. Not only were we going to have the little girl we so desperately wanted, we got to witness a cornerstone in our son's faith. He had prayed for a baby sister and God had answered him. While I knew his prayers would not always be so simplistic or be met with miraculous answers, I basked in the goodness of God to a little four-year-old boy, who had endured such hardships during his first year of life.

We couldn't wait to share the news with our friends and family. We planned a quick get together for the following day, inviting everyone into our backyard for the gender reveal. We filled a box with twenty pink balloons, carefully taping it shut before placing it in the back yard. With friends and family gathered round in person and on our phones, we let Harley help tear the box open.

Squeals and screams erupted through the trees as the pink balloons floated to the sky. Grandparents were crying while kids were screaming. After the sadness and heartache everyone had endured through my cancer journey, I was thrilled to bring such joy into their lives for a change.

The remaining weeks of my pregnancy were picture-perfect. I felt amazing and my doctors were pleasantly surprised by my progress and lack of complications. I finally got to wear some of the maternity clothes I never had had the chance to wear with Harley.

I went into labor on the morning of October 20. We made our way to the hospital with our parents and Krista meeting us there. As with Harley's delivery, things progressed quickly. My big hips worked in my favor again, aiding in the fast delivery, but did not allow time to correct a major issue. The epidural only numbed one side of my body. Before anything could be done, it was time to push.

In a way that only she could, Dr. Soundararajan simply said, "You're going to have to suck it up honey. This baby is coming."

Quick is always preferred during natural childbirth, even if it's only half natural. At 4:39PM, Grace Annabelle Hallford arrived, Gracie. We got to experience the joy of welcoming a child into the world without a cancer diagnosis and surgery looming.

Shortly after delivery, Harley climbed up on my bed and I placed Gracie, the little flower he had prayed for so long, in his arms. His face beamed as he posed for pictures and studied her little features. David stood beside us, his hand resting on my shoulder. As I reached around to grip his hand, I felt complete.

***

In early 2016, with Gracie now three and Harley eight, we began to consider the possibility of having another baby. Given the dismal odds of getting pregnant with Gracie, we assumed that there would be little to no chance of another baby. Lightning just couldn't strike twice, right?

Shortly after I was in remission, I noticed that I could still produce breast milk, despite having only nursed Harley for a just a few weeks. However, it wasn't until after the fog of detox had lifted that I thought to mention it to Dr. Miller. She referred me to an endocrinologist to have my prolactin hormone levels checked.

As suspected, my prolactin levels were high. The endocrinologist explained that since my body was lactating at the time of radiation, the radiation could have essentially crossed the wires in my brain, causing my body to maintain high levels of prolactin, which in turn would cause lifelong milk production. Awesome, I clearly needed to add a few chapters to the "what to expect from cancer" manual that had apparently been lost in the mail. He prescribed medication to help stop the milk production, which eventually helped after some dosage tweaking.

Since high levels of prolactin can sometimes lead to prolactinoma, a mass on the pituitary gland, I continued to see the endocrinologist for semi-annual checkups. I posed the pregnancy question to my endocrinologist at one of those appointments.

"It would be extremely difficult for you to conceive given your history," he confirmed, rolling his stool closer to my chair as he spoke. "Your thyroid levels are not ideal, and your prolactin levels remain high. I'm sorry, but it would be highly unlikely given those circumstances."

With two healthy kids, we knew we would not pursue fertility treatments or adoption this time. Another child would be icing on top of a pretty tall cake of blessings. We just decided to pray and let things happen naturally, content with the idea that it may not.

My annual brain MRI was scheduled for the following week. As the years passed, the concern over these scans began to decrease slightly, but they were still met with anxious anticipation. Since I had no monthly cycle, I had no way of knowing if I was pregnant without taking a pregnancy test. With regular scans and tests, I learned to keep a small stock of tests at home to take before any scans were performed.

I pulled out the test, took it and laid it on the counter. With my first pregnancy, I had held the stick in my hand, willing the lines to appear. I had no reason to believe I was pregnant now though, so I left the stick on the counter as I applied my makeup. As I picked up the stick, my breath caught. I reached for the wall to steady myself.

Two pink lines.

"This can't be right," I whispered to myself. I tapped my foot on the floor, pondering my next step. I reached back into the cabinet for another test.

Two pink lines.

Apparently, lightning can strike twice. I was floored, completely caught off guard. The Lord had once again defied all medical reasoning to give us another child, before we really even had a chance to seriously ask. The Lord had probably chuckled at my ovulation charts and tests the first time around when I thought I was in control, but he continued to show His goodness to us.

David's reaction mirrored mine when I told him later that afternoon. We planned to tell our kids and our parents the following weekend. We asked everyone to stop by the house on Friday evening. We had plans to go out to dinner and no one thought it unusual to meet at our house beforehand. I casually brought out a square box, wrapped in pink and blue polka-dots. I handed the gift to Gracie.

The corner of her lip turned up in a suspicious smile. Harley stood next to her as she peeled back the paper. My mom and Patsy sat behind Gracie on the sofa, the sunset light shining through the blinds behind them. Richard and my dad stood propped up against the doorway leading to the kitchen. Gracie pulled out a book, studying it carefully, as if for a moment, she thought she could read. Harley peered past her bundle of light brown hair to read the words for her.

"I'm Going to be a Big Sister." The words rolled off his tongue with no emotion. He read it again.

"I'm Going to Be a Big Sister!?" His voice rose in excitement with each word. He began jumping up and down. Gracie, completely clueless to the unfolding events, mimicked her brother's excitement and enthusiasm.

"What does this mean?" he squealed.

The excitement on one side of the room, failed to reach the other. Our moms sat speechless on the couch, their jaws practically scraping the rug where Lulu lay sleeping.

"What?? What did you say?" Harley held up the book for everyone to see.

The initial jolt of shock and concern was a bit jarring, but as the surprise wore off, the excitement grew. Tears flowed easily for our dads as we gave hugs all around.

My pregnancy progressed almost identically to the one with Gracie. I followed the same schedule of seeing my OB, Dr. Soundararajan, the high-risk OB doctor as well as my new oncologist, Dr. Long.

We missed Dr. Miller, who had moved out of state after Gracie was born. She had been an intricate part of our story and we had grown to be friends over the years. Her absence left a hole in my heart that no other doctor could ever really fill.

One benefit of having a baby after age 35 is a free genetic test. At the end of my first trimester I was surprised by the news that the test results contained the gender of our baby.

"Do you want to know what you are having?" the doctor asked, not sure if I would want to find out without David there. He was working a shift at the fire station. I hadn't even considered that I would find out the gender so soon.

"Sure, we want to know. I can call my husband and let him know." Funny how things change the third time around, compared to the cramped ultrasound room with Harley.

"It's a boy!"

I reached David after the appointment to tell him, and we decided to throw together an impromptu gender reveal. We were traveling to the beach after David's shift and didn't want to be stuck holding the secret in while we were away. I threw together a sign reading "Bows and Frills or Boats and Thrills," and grabbed some cans of blue silly string at the party store. Carefully wrapping the cans in duct tape to conceal the contents, I packed everything up and headed to the fire station that evening with the kids. Our families and David's co-workers stood around as we handed Harley and Gracie the cans of silly string. Blue string squirted on the ground at first but quickly found its way onto their faces and in their hair in the excitement.

On January, 20, 2017 I went to the labor and delivery floor one last time. The pregnancy had progressed like Gracie's with no complications. As I sat in the bed with the induction medications working their magic, we watched the Inauguration ceremony on TV. The political atmosphere of the day made for lively conversation among the staff. With a fully working epidural, I delivered our third baby, Eli David.

Two days later I walked in the door of our house, holding our new little man in my arms. A house that had been a home to two barely-grown-up kids with a dream to start a family of their own, who brought home a crazy dog. A house where a firefighter's wife learned to cook by burning quite a few meals and even setting the smoke detectors off a time or two. A house that had once been the scene of deep sadness and relentless pain. A house that heard the screams and cries to God on hard days and dark nights. A house that had been filled with the outpouring of love from a community of friends and family during such a desperate time.

The walls that had been laced with tears and sorrow now reverberated with the joys and giggles of three children.

We would watch all three of them roll over, sit up, crawl, and walk inside those four walls. I pictured many successful bike rides, hover board tricks, swing jumps, dance twirls, and gymnast flips at this house. I thought about the boo-boos that would happen on that driveway and the many pictures we could make on the front porch swing. Harley was almost old enough to help David hang the Christmas lights along the gutter in the winter and lay pine straw in the flower beds in the spring.

The house stood firm around a husband and wife as we pressed through the trials of life together and grew stronger through it all. Those walls represented our faith – strong and secure not because of our own strength, but because of the One who graciously gave us the strength to endure. Our home welcomed us like an old friend and provided a safe space to be a family. It was the storybook ending I could never have dreamed possible.

Of course, our cozy homecoming is not the end of the journey. The aftermath of cancer is its own physical challenge, and we've grown past expecting, or even wanting, a simple "happily ever after." We need better than "happy." We need the deep peace of joy in the Lord to sustain us through the ongoing health issues and whatever else may come.

Chapter 24
Remission Is Not the End

"...for I have learned, in whatsoever state I am, therewith to be content." Phi. 4: 11

Before I had personally experienced cancer, I assumed that when someone went into remission, his or her physical suffering was over. Unfortunately, for most people that is simply not the case. After speaking engagements, I am often asked if I have any lasting side effects. I jokingly reply, "If you want to hear them all, you had better pull up a chair." In response to those questions, I wanted to share lasting issues I deal with as a result of my cancer and treatments. If you have been through cancer, I know you can agree that it doesn't all end at remission.

A few milder side effects include dry mouth, dry eyes, low iron, and neuropathy. Since, the tumor wrapped around the glands in my neck, my doctors had to remove all the salivary glands on the right side. This leaves my mouth extremely dry. I have to have gum or water with me at all times to help keep my mouth from feeling like a cotton ball.

Adding to the facial moisture problems, my right tear duct doesn't produce tears. I have to constantly put prescription-strength artificial tears in my eye to keep it from drying out. This also leads to lack of tears. I can sometimes come across as cold in an emotionally charged situation where everyone is crying around me, but it is really just a literal lack of tears.

Neuropathy is a nerve condition that can lead to pain and tingling, for me, especially in my hands and feet. It also causes sensitivity to temperatures. For example, if David and I were to touch the same pan, he would say it was warm to the touch, while it would feel burning hot to me. Any exposure to extreme temperatures exacerbates these symptoms.

Before I had cancer, allergies were never an issue for me. I wasn't allergic to any foods or medications. Now I have a long list of allergies! One doctor explained that since chemo kills good cells along with harmful ones, sometimes the good cells rebuild with a completely different cell structure. After a series of hive-ridden allergic reactions, Dr. Miller recommended I undergo allergy testing to get more information. The allergist performed the standard back pricking test, as well as food patch tests. This disgusting process included wearing small patches of food on my back for 48 hours. It is as gross as it sounds. In addition to the medication and dyes I was already aware of, I found out that I had developed allergies to mustard, oats, and to a lesser degree dairy and potatoes.

The more severe side effects that impact my daily life more significantly are esophagus restriction, high prolactin levels, head pain, trigeminal neuralgia, and hearing loss.

Due to the damage to my throat from the radiation treatments, I have to have my esophagus dilated every 6-12 months. I know it is time to have the procedure again when eating becomes an issue. I frequently find myself choking on food, as my throat shrivels back down over the course of a few months. Thankfully all of the procedures since the first one have been uneventful!

The temporary tube that Dr. Parks placed in my right ear after radiation treatments is now unfortunately permanently fixed in place. Due to this, I have to be careful to avoid getting water in my ears. Despite my best efforts, I often develop ear infections due to the bacteria highway now forever placed in my ear.

More concerning however is the loss of hearing in my right ear. Simply not being able to hear out of it would be troublesome enough, but I experience constant static noise. It is a like my ear perpetually sits on a bad radio station! Friends and family have grown accustomed to talking to me either face to face or on my left side. They know that if the right side of my head is turned toward them, I won't be able to hear a thing!

During my treatments, two major sources of pain were headaches, due to the brain tumor, and bone pain, due to the shots I received after chemotherapy. After treatments ended, the bone pain subsided, but the headaches remained. The intensity of the pain decreased and changed, but never went away. In 2010, with the detox process complete, the pain became increasingly evident in my daily activities.

"It is not like a regular headache," I explained to Dr. Spector during a routine visit. "It feels different. It is a deep pain. Deeper than any headache I have ever felt." A clear MRI scan ruled out the possibility of a brain tumor. With such vague symptoms, he started with a straight forward pain management approach. Over the next few years, he prescribed a variety of oral medications and injections to help combat the pain. None of the medicine helped and most of it left me feeling groggy. After going through such a dramatic detox experience, I struggled with the idea of taking any medication, and refused take anything that made me feel groggy or dazed. I resolved to just deal with the pain rather than take medication that made me feel drugged.

Dr. Miller suggested that the head pain could be linked to anxiety. While I had never been diagnosed with any anxiety disorders, I did struggle with anxiety over the cancer returning. Every bump, lump, or symptom I experienced, I immediately attributed to my cancer returning. David and my mom had a right to call me a hypochondriac. Dr. Miller prescribed Ativan, an anxiety medication. Like the medications from Dr. Spector, it had no effect on my symptoms.

Around the time Gracie was born in 2012, Dr. Spector retired, and Dr. Miller moved out of state. In a few months' time, I lost the two primary doctors on my complex medical case. One night, I curled up next to David on the couch and cried. I felt lost. Finding two new doctors and building relationships of trust seemed too overwhelming. A new oncologist had to be the first step.

After reviewing my case and assessing my head pain, Dr. Long, my new oncologist, referred me to a pain management doctor. He suggested a procedure called a Sphenopalatine Ganglion Block. The procedure would involve inserting a large tube in my nose and reaching the edge of my brain to block a nerve that may be causing the pain. I reluctantly agreed, desperate for any relief.

As I entered the procedure room at the pain clinic, a gentleman I had never met approached me and introduced himself.

"Hello, I'm Steve. I'm a company representative for the machine your doctor will be using today. Since this is his first time attempting this procedure…."

I didn't hear anything after the words "first time." If I didn't have an anxiety problem before, I did now. I gazed at the door, calculating if it was too late to run. Ignoring my screaming sense and gut feelings to bolt, I inched myself into the chair and gripped the arm rests.

"We will know right away if this works. The relief is instantaneous." His peppy tone did not quell my feelings. I was about to let a novice insert a tube up my nose, to my brain, and mess with a nerve. Given my worst-case-scenario medical record, I couldn't believe my body was still sitting in the chair.

The doctor was correct in his assessment – we did know the result right away. It didn't help at all. Coupled with the excruciating pain of the procedure, I felt the exact opposite of immediate relief. I left the office with no less head pain, annoyance at a waste of time and money, and one enlarged nostril.

The next month at a routine ENT appointment with Dr. Parks to monitor the tube in my right ear, I told him about the procedure with the pain doctor. He graciously recommended a new neurologist, assuring me that would be the surest road to an answer and relief. Apparently, I was not the only one in Atlanta who wanted to see this doctor. I was placed on the wait list and told it may be *years* before an appointment opened up.

During the long wait to get an appointment, additional symptoms popped up, and the intensity of the headache flare-ups increased. Some days the headaches would be minor, while other days, they would force me to bed. Then episodes began with my face drawing to one side, mimicking a stroke victim's symptoms. My face would be paralyzed in that position for ten to fifteen seconds before releasing. My face hurt and, like my hands and toes, grew sensitive to temperature changes.

In 2015, a new patient appointment finally opened up with the new neurologist, Dr. Smith. I had researched my symptoms for years at this point and after a lengthy introduction and medical history, I blurted out, "Could this be trigeminal neuralgia?" inwardly cringing at what I feared would be a butchering pronunciation of the medical terminology.

After pausing to review my symptoms again, he agreed. "That could definitely be a possibility given your history. Your brain tumor was located next to your trigeminal nerve and could have certainly caused damage to it," he explained, pointing to a diagram of the brain hanging on the wall.

He put me on medication designed to alleviate the symptoms of trigeminal neuralgia, but of course, I had an allergic reaction. I had come to expect that any time I took a pill! Dr. Smith advised a different medication to try along with Botox treatments. Now that was one treatment I would not fight against! However, before the new medication could be prescribed or the Botox treatments could begin, I found out I was pregnant with Eli.

Living to see my children grow and remaining alongside my husband and family is worth any side effect that the cancer and treatments may have caused. I am thankful for each day and do not take my time on earth for granted. I am thankful for the medical advancements and wise doctors that God used to save my life. However, I feel the after-effects chapter is an important part of the story to share so that others don't make the same assumption that I did: that it all ends at remission. Anticipating lasting and sometimes life altering side effects after hearing the news, "You're cancer free," can benefit patients as well as family members, friends and caregivers.

Chapter 25
Impossible Odds

*"Who comforteth us in all our tribulation, that we may be able
to comfort them which are in any trouble, by the comfort
wherewith we ourselves are comforted by God." II Cor. 1:4*

God could clearly see a future for this story that I
could have never imagined. He saw that He could use my
notoriously big mouth for a greater purpose. As II
Corinthians 1:4 tells us, God allowed us to go through a
trial in order to be able to comfort others. I have tried to
take every opportunity to share my story in hopes of
providing comfort to others and to give God glory for my
life.

In 2009, I received my first speaking request. A
medical group wanted me to come share my story on a
conference call during their lunch hour. I felt inadequate
to tell my stories to a bunch of doctors, knowing I would
probably mess up some of the medical lingo. I prayed and
submitted my heart to be obedient to the opportunity and
let the Lord shape the outcome. I was blown away with
the response to my story. Soon more speaking requests,
mostly from churches and ladies' groups, streamed in.

Now, over almost a decade, I have been able to
share my story with thousands of people in person and
millions more through online and media appearances. In

the spring of 2017, after speaking to over 2,000 women at a women's conference, a lady attending the conference wrote an article detailing my story that got picked up by the Associated Press. The article spread like wildfire through mainstream news organizations like *The Today Show*, *People*, *Redbook*, and ABC. In the fall of 2017, my story was featured on *The 700 Club*. In May of 2018, David, Dr. Miller and I were flown to New York City to appear on Megyn Kelly Today. God has blown the doors off the box of expectations I imagined for where He could take this story.

This book is even a picture of God's sovereignty in my story. Given the eye problems I continue to struggle with, I knew that I would never be able to write this story on my own, yet I felt like God wanted me to write a book. So, I did what I had learned to do when doors seemed to be closed – I prayed. I prayed specifically that God would open an avenue for a book to be written. Days later, a family friend approached me about ghost writing my story. She had been praying about approaching me for a few weeks. Once again, God had orchestrated events in His time far beyond what I could have ever imagined.

I can honestly say that I wouldn't trade cancer for the life I had before. I don't wish cancer upon anyone, but I am thankful for what it has done in my life. I know God in an intimate personal way that I didn't before. He isn't just a someone that we talk about on Sunday or a Santa Claus in the sky that takes requests.

I pray differently now than I did before. My prayer life was casual at best. Now I understand that prayer is an unmatched force of power in any situation. James 5:16 assures us that "the effectual fervent prayer of a righteous man availeth much." David and I understand the power of prayer and take it seriously when we are asked to pray about a situation. We often stop and immediately pray when we hear about a situation or person that needs prayer. Before, prayer was a thing we did, now it is a way of life. I acknowledge my dependence on God every hour of the day through prayer. (Can any other mommas give a witness? Every. Single. Hour.) Pray big and pray specifically! Don't think any prayer is too hard or too big for God!

The most enduring shift in my life has been a sense of hope. Philippians 4:6-7 shows us that through prayer comes an unshakeable hope and peace in Christ. When we lay our heartaches down at His feet in prayer – sickness, unemployment, finances, marriages that seem hopeless, rebellious kids – we cry out to a God who is sovereign and who is good. When we leave the burdens there, trusting Him to meet the need, heal the friend, mend the marriage, or rescue the child, we are promised a sweet peace. Not a peace that everything will work out the way we hoped. Many people die from cancer, especially stage-four lung cancer. Your story may not turn out exactly like mine. Maybe your mom died or your sister never came back. Yet the promise of peace remains. See, the peace isn't that the storm will be calmed. The peace and the hope is that we can trust that He will never leave us or forsake us in the wind and rain.

David: *In II Kings 20, King Hezekiah was sick. In fact, Isaiah told him he was going to die. Despite his death sentence directly from God, he prayed. He didn't call his family or friends. He didn't whine and moan at his fate. His immediate response was prayer and he prayed in the face of impossible odds. Before Isaiah even got out the door, God told him to turn around and tell Hezekiah his prayer had been answered. He would live.*

Throughout Ashley's illness I prayed. Our family, friends, and church prayed as well. I wasn't sure what God was going to do in our story, but I knew God is no respecter of persons. I knew He could heal Ashley just like he healed Hezekiah, so that's what I prayed with a childlike faith. I just believed God was who He said He was and could do what He said He would do.

Our prayer is that you would walk away from this story with the same resolve. Prayer is a powerful weapon that God gives us to face the trials in this life. Don't ever assume that a situation is too far gone for Him to work.

If you are facing a cancer diagnosis or have someone close to you that is, the best advice I can give is to build a support system. Reach out to family, friends, and a local church. Our story would not have been the same without a strong network of people supporting us. Also, embrace what the Lord can teach you through your difficult circumstances. Someone out there needs to hear your story and see how God worked in your life. Don't miss an opportunity to be a blessing to other people.

Sheila: *Every cancer diagnosis is different, tailor-made to that individual and family. What works for one situation may not work for another, but everyone needs support when faced with something so tragic. I felt helpless as Ashley's mom. I wanted to fix it, but being able to step in and help take care of her and Harley gave me something to focus on rather than just sit around and worry all the time.*

Outside of watching Ashley and her family suffer, the most difficult part of the ordeal for me was being isolated from family and friends. Since I essentially moved in with Ashley and David, I even struggled to stay connected with my husband and son. Since the house needed to stay as quiet as possible due to Ashley's extreme pain, phone calls and visitors were kept at a minimum, creating an unintentional secluded bubble around us all. Some friends drifted away because they didn't fully understand the circumstances, but I am so thankful for the ones that stayed by my side and offered help, even from a distance.

If you have a loved one going through cancer, the best thing you can do is be a friend and offer your support. Many well-meaning people offered truckloads of advice on everything from medications to doctors. Since few people talked directly to Ashley, we were left to absorb the information ourselves. Most of the time, families don't need medical advice or suggestions. They just need a hug and a prayer. They feel overwhelmed, and in the crashing waves of bad news, sometimes they don't even know what they need. Simple suggestions help a lot. Like, "Hey, could I bring dinner tonight?" instead of "Let me know if I can do anything." People from our church provided meals, prayers, and weekly care packages with things like laundry detergent, diapers, formula, and cleaning supplies. They were our lifeline in the darkest days.

Patsy: *No one writes a manual for how to deal with cancer. Most of the time, especially as the in-laws, we were on the outside looking in to the medical decisions and family dynamic. We didn't always know the right thing to do, but we could always pray. We prayed about everything – for Ashley's health to be restored, for David's strength, for endurance for our family, and for wisdom in dealing with every situation. If you are facing a trial, don't believe the lie that you are alone. Even if you have no one to turn to, God will hear your prayers.*

Even though it was one of the worst spiritual valleys I had traveled, through faith, I could focus on the mountain tops of God's goodness, despite our circumstances. I look back now and realize how it increased my faith. Now I can honestly say it was a privilege and blessing to have been in this valley as a family.

Krista: *I remember going back to work after being home for the holidays and learning that the cancer had spread. I had taken care of two babies the night before, and although ICU can be unpredictable, I looked forward to continuing the care of patients I already knew. When I arrived at work that night, however, my assignment had been changed to accommodate a NICU nurse who floated to work in our unit. Understandable? Yes, but in that moment, I experienced upheaval in an area of my life where I thought I would have a little bit of consistency. My grief from my personal life spilled over into that moment as tears fell down my face, shocking my coworkers I'm sure. It's important to process your grief and not keep it bottled up inside. I tell my patients' parents this all the time: "Take care of yourself so that you can take care of your baby." You might not be the one fighting cancer, but watching someone you love go through that is hard.*

So, if you find yourself reading this and are wondering how you can help someone with cancer, I say just love them. Strive to focus on the actual person and not so much on the cancer. Live in the moment. Savor the good ones and soak up time with your person. Push through the bad days because a good one is around the corner. Recognize those grace moments. The moments when you can't help but know that God is there. Be there for your loved one, in whatever way they need you to be. Provide a listening ear when they need it. Be a shoulder to cry on when they need it. Bring some laughter to their life when they need it. Let them know that it is okay to feel how they are feeling. They don't have to be strong 24/7. It's okay to laugh. It's okay to cry. It's okay to be angry. It's okay to be scared. It's okay to want to sit in silence. If you can't be there in person, send them a card. You never know when they might need to see a word of encouragement. Pray with them. Pray for them. Surround yourself with people who you can count on to pray with you. Maybe that's not your thing, but I can't help but take away the power of prayer in this situation. Thoughts and prayers sentiments tend to sometimes be cliché these days, but I strive to be intentional with this. I know what a difference it can make. We have seen it work first hand through Ashley's life.

Brother Eddie: *Abraham and Isaac walked alone on their journey to the mountain to make the sacrifice God had instructed Abraham to make. No matter how closely we read their story, we will never be able to feel the burden they felt that day. As you watch someone go through a trial, you can never fully appreciate what is going on in their lives; however, you can help share the load. Pray for them and ask how you can help. Most people won't ask for help, but in these types of situations, anyone could use a meal, a few hours of childcare, or a note of encouragement.*

I pray that this story inspires you to never give up, to never see a situation as hopeless, beyond the reach of an all-powerful God. God didn't resurrect Job's kids from the dead when he restored his health and possessions.

Through all the pain and hopelessness he must have felt, God resurrected new life and gave Job a more abundant life than He had before. That's what God does. He takes the ashes of our brokenness and births new life in the most unexpected places.

I would have loved to hear a post-trial interview with Job, say five or ten years down the road.

"So, Job, looks like things are going well! You are healthy, you have more possessions than you did before, and look at all these beautiful little kids running around! Your friends gather around your table and celebrate with you. Life seems good! So, why do you think all those things happened to you? Ten years later do you have a better understanding of why?"

"Because He's God and I'm not."

Blink. Blink. Blink.

"That's it? That's enough of an answer for you?"

"Yeah. That's it. When you really understand it, it is enough. He's God. I can trust that He is good and powerful and sovereign beyond anything I could imagine. He is in control. He suspends the entire universe in His hand. All I have to do is trust. Seems like a pretty good deal to me.

An Invitation

If someone came to you and offered you a $100 bill, would you look at them and say, "No thanks. I'm good."? No, you would snatch that up in a heartbeat. The Bible tells us in Ephesians 2:8-9, "For by grace are ye saved through faith; and that not of yourselves: it is the gift of God: Not of works, lest any man should boast."

Jesus Christ is offering so much more than $100 bill. He is offering you an eternal home in Heaven with him and sparing you from eternal torment in Hell.
Jesus said, "I am the way, the truth, and the life: no man cometh unto the Father, but by me." John 14:6

1. You need to admit you are a sinner. Romans 3:10 "As it is written, there is none righteous, no, not one:"
2. You need to be willing to turn from your sin and repent. Acts 17:30, "And the times of this ignorance God winked at; but now commandeth all men everywhere to repent:"
3. You need to believe that Jesus Christ died for you, was buried, and rose from the dead. Romans 10:9-10, "That if thou shalt confess with thy mouth the Lord Jesus, and shalt believe in thine heart that God hath raised him from the dead, thou shalt be saved. For with the heart man believeth unto righteousness; and with the mouth confession is made unto salvation."
4. You need to pray and invite Jesus into your life to become your personal Savior. Romans 10:13, "For whosoever shall call upon the name of the Lord shall be saved."

If you are ready to do that, then you can simply pray a prayer similar to this:

"Dear Lord, I know that I am a sinner and need Your forgiveness. I do believe that Jesus Christ died on the cross and shed His precious blood for my sin. I am ready and willing to turn from my sin. Lord, please come into my heart and save me today."

Once you have prayed, I encourage you to tell someone. You should look for a local church to join and engage with other believers. Read your Bible daily and study it. The Lord will speak to you through His Word.

This is the best decision you will ever make in your life!

Acknowledgments

Ashley

Harley – My firstborn. You made me a mom. I had no idea my heart could love another person so much. You came into the world, and we walked into the darkest days of my life. I'm so thankful God gave you to me. You were a ray of sunshine during those dark days, and I know that having you made me fight so much harder. You are so precious to me. I will love you forever and always! Joshua 1:9

Gracie- My pretty princess. When I was young, I knew I wanted to be a mom, and I knew I wanted a little girl. I prayed God would give me a girl so I could have a shopping buddy, a pedicure partner, and someone to watch all the princess movies with. When God gave me you, He answered all those prayers! You are so precious to me. I will love you forever and always! Proverbs 31:30

Eli- My little caboose. You completed our family. Your smile is contagious and everyone who meets you, loves you. I love watching you explore the world around you and being able to see things through your eyes. I thank God for blessing us with you. You keep me on my toes and keep me young! You are so precious to me. I will love you forever and always! Proverbs 3:5-6

David – There is no way I will ever be able to thank you for everything you have done for me and the support you have given to me. I am so blessed to have you as my husband. I thank God for you and for the way He drew us closer because of my illness. I love you more than you'll ever know.

Dad and Mom – I cannot imagine the pain you both felt during my illness. I thank you both for being strong for me and for being there for whatever was needed. You both sacrificed so much to be able to

312

lighten our load, and I will never forget it. I thank God for giving me the best parents in the world. I love you both so very much!

Richard and Patsy – I am so thankful for such wonderful in-laws. You both have always treated me like your very own and I am very thankful for that. Thank you for the sacrifices you both made in order to help ease our burden. I will never forget everything you did for me. I love you both very much!

Joshua, Nathan, and Krista – Thank you for all the fundraising, calls, texts, late night Starbucks runs, and love you showed us. Krista, you were our nurse on duty at all times. I don't know how we would've made it without having you there to help take care of Harley. Nathan, thank you for being there for
David and loaning out Krista to us so many times. Joshua, thank you for organizing donut sales and for stopping whatever you were doing to bring me a Starbucks! You are all loved very much!

Stephanie – You took a dream I've had for many years and made it come true. I will never forget praying and asking God if He wanted a book written to send me the help I needed. Within a week or so, you reached out to me. I know this process has been extremely difficult at times. I am beyond thankful for the sacrifices you have made to make this book happen. I am incredibly blessed to call you my friend!

Lisa – Thank you so very much for your help and guidance throughout this process. Your suggestions were always right, even if I didn't see it at first. You are very talented and I'm so thankful God brought you in on this project.

Nic – You came in at the end of this and were a lifesaver. I do not have any idea what we would've done without your knowledge and help. Thank you for sacrificing your time and working so quickly to help us get this book published.

Phillip - Thank you for handling the website and arranging links for book orders. I truly appreciate your knowledge and help.

To all of my family, friends, and church family – There is no way I could ever say thank you enough. Thank you for the calls, texts, cards, food, donations, and most important, prayers. Your prayers changed my life. Thank you from the bottom of my heart. I love you all.

Stephanie

Ashley – Thank you for trusting me to write your story. I am forever humbled and grateful for your confidence in me to handle such precious memories. Thank you for your grace and patience with my unending questions and accidental chapters. I cannot wait to see what the Lord has planned!

Lisa – This project simply wouldn't be here without you. The Lord knew I needed you! Your firm but gentle hand helped me tell this story with the power and depth that it deserved. You also made me laugh at times when all I wanted to do was cry! Thank you for mentoring, teaching, coaching and supporting me along the way.

Chad – Thank you for stepping up to fill in the gaps and make it easy for me to write. Thank you for letting me write out loud and for encouraging me each step of the way. I love you!

Addison, Mya, Lucy, and Jake – I love you guys more than you could ever know. Addison, thank you for taking the perfect headshot. Addison and Mya, thank you for making lunches, cleaning, and keeping the wheels on the bus so that I could have time to write. You guys cheered me on, even when I felt like I would never finish. I hope all four of you see this project as an inspiration to never doubt what the Lord can do in your lives. Love Jesus and dream big!

Natalie, Leigh, Krista and Monica – Thank you for reading and rereading and always giving me honest answers. I always need that!

Pastor Barry Parks – Thank you for challenging me to dream again.

For more information and speaking engagement requests, visit www.ashleyhallford.com

Follow Ashley Hallford on Facebook and Instagram (@ adhallford) for the latest news and updates.